THE PELICAN SHAKESPEARE
GENERAL EDITORS

STEPHEN ORGEL
A. R. BRAUNMULLER

The History of Troilus and Cressida

Cressida gives Diomedes Troilus's love token (V.2), watched
by Ulysses, Troilus, and Thersites. Frontispiece to the play in
Nicholas Rowe's Shakespeare, 1709, the first illustrated
edition. The play is imagined on an early-eighteenth-century
stage. The men are in Roman armor, but Cressida is
costumed as a contemporary London courtesan.

William Shakespeare

The History of
Troilus and Cressida

EDITED BY JONATHAN CREWE

PENGUIN BOOKS

PENGUIN BOOKS
Published by the Penguin Group
Penguin Putnam Inc., 375 Hudson Street,
New York, New York 10014, U.S.A.
Penguin Books Ltd, 27 Wrights Lane,
London W8 5TZ, England
Penguin Books Australia Ltd, Ringwood,
Victoria, Australia
Penguin Books Canada Ltd, 10 Alcorn Avenue,
Toronto, Ontario, Canada M4V 3B2
Penguin Books (N.Z.) Ltd, 182–190 Wairau Road,
Auckland 10, New Zealand

Penguin Books Ltd, Registered Offices:
Harmondsworth, Middlesex, England

The History of Troilus and Cressida edited by Virgil K. Whitaker
published in the United States of America in Penguin Books 1958
Revised edition published 1970
This new edition edited by Jonathan Crewe published 2000

3   5   7   9   10   8   6   4

Copyright © Penguin Books Inc., 1958, 1970
Copyright © Penguin Putnam Inc., 2000
All rights reserved

ISBN 0-14-07.1486 3
(CIP data available)

Printed in the United States of America
Set in Adobe Garamond
Designed by Virginia Norey

Contents

Publisher's Note

IT IS ALMOST half a century since the first volumes of the Pelican Shakespeare appeared under the general editorship of Alfred Harbage. The fact that a new edition, rather than simply a revision, has been undertaken reflects the profound changes textual and critical studies of Shakespeare have undergone in the past twenty years. For the new Pelican series, the texts of the plays and poems have been thoroughly revised in accordance with recent scholarship, and in some cases have been entirely reedited. New introductions and notes have been provided in all the volumes. But the new Shakespeare is also designed as a successor to the original series; the previous editions have been taken into account, and the advice of the previous editors has been solicited where it was feasible to do so.

Certain textual features of the new Pelican Shakespeare should be particularly noted. All lines are numbered that contain a word, phrase, or allusion explained in the glossarial notes. In addition, for convenience, every tenth line is also numbered, in italics when no annotation is indicated. The intrusive and often inaccurate place headings inserted by early editors are omitted (as is becoming standard practice), but for the convenience of those who miss them, an indication of locale now appears as the first item in the annotation of each scene.

In the interest of both elegance and utility, each speech prefix is set in a separate line when the speaker's lines are in verse, except when those words form the second half of a verse line. Thus the verse form of the speech is kept visually intact. What is printed as verse and what is printed as prose has, in general, the authority of the original texts. Departures from the original texts in this regard have only the authority of editorial tradition and the judgment of the Pelican editors; and, in a few instances, are admittedly arbitrary.

The Theatrical World

ECONOMIC REALITIES determined the theatrical world in which Shakespeare's plays were written, performed, and received. For centuries in England, the primary theatrical tradition was nonprofessional. Craft guilds (or "mysteries") provided religious drama – mystery plays – as part of the celebration of religious and civic festivals, and schools and universities staged classical and neoclassical drama in both Latin and English as part of their curricula. In these forms, drama was established and socially acceptable. Professional theater, in contrast, existed on the margins of society. The acting companies were itinerant; playhouses could be any available space – the great halls of the aristocracy, town squares, civic halls, inn yards, fair booths, or open fields – and income was sporadic, dependent on the passing of the hat or on the bounty of local patrons. The actors, moreover, were considered little better than vagabonds, constantly in danger of arrest or expulsion.

In the late 1560s and 1570s, however, English professional theater began to gain respectability. Wealthy aristocrats fond of drama – the Lord Admiral, for example, or the Lord Chamberlain – took acting companies under their protection so that the players technically became members of their households and were no longer subject to arrest as homeless or masterless men. Permanent theaters were first built at this time as well, allowing the companies to control and charge for entry to their performances.

Shakespeare's livelihood, and the stunning artistic explosion in which he participated, depended on pragmatic and architectural effort. Professional theater requires ways to restrict access to its offerings; if it does not, and admission fees cannot be charged, the actors do not get paid, the costumes go to a pawnbroker, and there is no such thing as a professional, ongoing theatrical tradition. The answer to that economic need arrived in the late 1560s and 1570s with the creation of the so-called public or amphitheater playhouse. Recent discoveries indicate that the precursor of the Globe playhouse in London (where Shakespeare's mature plays were presented) and the Rose theater (which presented Christopher Marlowe's plays and some of Shakespeare's earliest ones) was the Red Lion theater of 1567. Archaeological studies of the foundations of the Rose and Globe theaters have revealed that the open-air theater of the 1590s and later was probably a polygonal building with fourteen to twenty or twenty-four sides, multistoried, from 75 to 100 feet in diameter, with a raised, partly covered "thrust" stage that projected into a group of standing patrons, or "groundlings," and a covered gallery, seating up to 2,500 or more (very crowded) spectators.

These theaters might have been about half full on any given day, though the audiences were larger on holidays or when a play was advertised, as old and new were, through printed playbills posted around London. The metropolitan area's late-Tudor, early-Stuart population (circa 1590–1620) has been estimated at about 150,000 to 250,000. It has been supposed that in the mid-1590s there were about 15,000 spectators per week at the public theaters; thus, as many as 10 percent of the local population went to the theater regularly. Consequently, the theaters' repertories – the plays available for this experienced and frequent audience – had to change often: in the month between September 15 and October 15, 1595, for instance, the Lord Admiral's Men performed twenty-eight times in eighteen different plays.

Since natural light illuminated the amphitheaters' stages, performances began between noon and two o'clock and ran without a break for two or three hours. They often concluded with a jig, a fencing display, or some other nondramatic exhibition. Weather conditions deter-

mined the season for the amphitheaters: plays were performed every day (including Sundays, sometimes, to cler-
ical dismay) except during Lent – the forty days before
Easter – or periods of plague, or sometimes during the
summer months when law courts were not in session and
the most affluent members of the audience were not in
London.

To a modern theatergoer, an amphitheater stage like
that of the Rose or Globe would appear an unfamiliar mixture of plainness and elaborate decoration. Much of the
structure was carved or painted, sometimes to imitate
marble; elsewhere, as under the canopy projecting over the
stage, to represent the stars and the zodiac. Appropriate
painted canvas pictures (of Jerusalem, for example, if the
play was set in that city) were apparently hung on the wall
behind the acting area, and tragedies were accompanied by
black hangings, presumably something like crepe festoons
or bunting. Although these theaters did not employ what
we would call scenery, early modern spectators saw numerous large props, such as the "bar" at which a prisoner stood
during a trial, the "mossy bank" where lovers reclined,
an arbor for amorous conversation, a chariot, gallows,
tables, trees, beds, thrones, writing desks, and so forth.
Audiences might learn a scene's location from a sign (reading "Athens," for example) carried across the stage (as in
Bertolt Brecht's twentieth-century productions). Equally
captivating (and equally irritating to the theater's enemies)
were the rich costumes and personal props the actors used:
the most valuable items in the surviving theatrical invento-
ries are the swords, gowns, robes, crowns, and other items
worn or carried by the performers.

Magic appealed to Shakespeare's audiences as much as
it does to us today, and the theater exploited many decep-
tive and spectacular devices. A winch in the loft above the
stage, called "the heavens," could lower and raise actors
playing gods, goddesses, and other supernatural figures to
and from the main acting area, just as one or more trap-
doors permitted entrances and exits to and from the area,

called "hell," beneath the stage. Actors wore elementary makeup such as wigs, false beards, and face paint, and they employed pig's bladders filled with animal blood to make wounds seem more real. They had rudimentary but effective ways of pretending to behead or hang a person. Supernumeraries (stagehands or actors not needed in a particular scene) could make thunder sounds (by shaking a metal sheet or rolling an iron ball down a chute) and show lightning (by blowing inflammable resin through tubes into a flame). Elaborate fireworks enhanced the effects of dragons flying through the air or imitated such celestial phenomena as comets, shooting stars, and multiple suns. Horses' hoofbeats, bells (located perhaps in the tower above the stage), trumpets and drums, clocks, cannon shots and gunshots, and the like were common sound effects. And the music of viols, cornets, oboes, and recorders was a regular feature of theatrical performances.

For two relatively brief spans, from the late 1570s to 1590 and from 1599 to 1614, the amphitheaters competed with the so-called private, or indoor, theaters, which originated as, or later represented themselves as, educational institutions training boys as singers for church services and court performances. These indoor theaters had two features that were distinct from the amphitheaters': their personnel and their playing spaces. The amphitheaters' adult companies included both adult men, who played the male roles, and boys, who played the female roles; the private, or indoor, theater companies, on the other hand, were entirely composed of boys aged about 8 to 16, who were, or could pretend to be, candidates for singers in a church or a royal boys' choir. (Until 1660, professional theatrical companies included no women.) The playing space would appear much more familiar to modern audiences than the long-vanished amphitheaters; the later indoor theaters were, in fact, the ancestors of the typical modern theater. They were enclosed spaces, usually rectangular, with the stage filling one end of the rectangle and the audience arrayed in seats or benches across (and sometimes lining) the building's longer axis. These spaces staged plays less frequently than the public theaters (perhaps only once a week) and held far fewer spectators than the amphitheaters: about 200 to 600, as opposed to 2,500 or more. Fewer patrons mean a smaller gross income, unless each pays more. Not surprisingly, then, private theaters charged higher prices than the amphitheaters, probably sixpence, as opposed to a penny for the cheapest entry.

Protected from the weather, the indoor theaters presented plays later in the day than the amphitheaters, and used artificial illumination – candles in sconces or candelabra. But candles melt, and need replacing, snuffing, and trimming, and these practical requirements may have been part of the reason the indoor theaters introduced breaks in the performance, the intermission so dear to the heart of theatergoers and to the pocketbooks of theater concessionaires ever since. Whether motivated by the need to tend to the candles or by the entrepreneurs' wishing to sell oranges and liquor, or both, the indoor theaters eventually established the modern convention of the noncontinuous performance. In the early modern "private" theater, musical performances apparently filled the intermissions, which in Stuart theater jargon seem to have been called "acts."

At the end of the first decade of the seventeenth century, the distinction between public amphitheaters and private indoor companies ceased. For various cultural, political, and economic reasons, individual companies gained control of both the public, open-air theaters and the indoor ones, and companies mixing adult men and boys took over the formerly "private" theaters. Despite the death of the boys' companies and of their highly innovative theaters (for which such luminous playwrights as Ben Jonson, George Chapman, and John Marston wrote), their playing spaces and conventions had an immense impact on subsequent plays: not merely for the intervals (which stressed the artistic and architectonic importance of "acts"), but also because they introduced political and social satire as a popular dramatic ingredient, even in tragedy, and a wider range of actorly effects, encouraged by their more intimate playing spaces.

Even the briefest sketch of the Shakespearean theatrical world would be incomplete without some comment on the social and cultural dimensions of theaters and playing in the period. In an intensely hierarchical and status-conscious society, professional actors and their ventures had hardly any respectability; as we have indicated, to protect themselves against laws designed to curb vagabondage and the increase of masterless men, actors resorted to the near-fiction that they were the servants of noble masters, and wore their distinctive livery. Hence the company for which Shakespeare wrote in the 1590s called itself the Lord Chamberlain's Men and pretended that the public, money-getting performances were in fact rehearsals for private performances before that high court official. From 1598, the Privy Council had licensed theatrical companies, and after 1603, with the accession of King James I, the companies gained explicit royal protection, just as the Queen's Men had for a time under Queen Elizabeth. The Chamberlain's Men became the King's Men, and the other companies were patronized by the other members of the royal family.

These designations were legal fictions that half-concealed an important economic and social development, the evolution away from the theater's organization on the model of the guild, a self-regulating confraternity of individual artisans, into a proto-capitalist organization. Shakespeare's company became a joint-stock company, where persons who supplied capital and, in some cases, such as Shakespeare's, capital and talent, employed themselves and others in earning a return on that capital. This development meant that actors and theater companies were outside both the traditional guild structures, which required some form of civic or royal charter, and the feudal household organization of master-and-servant. This anomalous, maverick social and economic condition made theater companies practically unruly and potentially even dangerous; consequently, numerous official bodies – including the London metropolitan and ecclesiastical authorities as well as, occasionally, the royal court itself – tried, without much success, to control and even to disband them.

Public officials had good reason to want to close the theaters: they were attractive nuisances – they drew often riotous crowds, they were always noisy, and they could be politically offensive and socially insubordinate. Until the Civil War, however, anti-theatrical forces failed to shut down professional theater, for many reasons – limited surveillance and few police powers, tensions or outright hostilities among the agencies that sought to check or channel theatrical activity, and lack of clear policies for control. Another reason must have been the theaters' undeniable popularity. Curtailing any activity enjoyed by such a substantial percentage of the population was difficult, as various Roman emperors attempting to limit circuses had learned, and the Tudor-Stuart audience was not merely large, it was socially diverse and included women. The prevalence of public entertainment in this period has been underestimated. In fact, fairs, holidays, games, sporting events, the equivalent of modern parades, freak shows, and street exhibitions all abounded, but the theater was the most widely and frequently available entertainment to which people of every class had access. That fact helps account both for its quantity and for the fear and anger it aroused.

WILLIAM SHAKESPEARE OF STRATFORD-UPON-AVON, GENTLEMAN

Many people have said that we know very little about William Shakespeare's life – pinheads and postcards are often mentioned as appropriately tiny surfaces on which to record the available information. More imaginatively and perhaps more correctly, Ralph Waldo Emerson wrote, "Shakespeare is the only biographer of Shakespeare. . . . So far from Shakespeare's being the least known, he is the one person in all modern history fully known to us."

In fact, we know more about Shakespeare's life than we do about almost any other English writer's of his era. His last will and testament (dated March 25, 1616) survives, as do numerous legal contracts and court documents involving Shakespeare as principal or witness, and parish records in Stratford and London. Shakespeare appears quite often in official records of King James's royal court, and of course Shakespeare's name appears on numerous title pages and in the written and recorded words of his literary contemporaries Robert Greene, Henry Chettle, Francis Meres, John Davies of Hereford, Ben Jonson, and many others. Indeed, if we make due allowance for the bloating of modern, run-of-the-mill bureaucratic records, more information has survived over the past four hundred years about William Shakespeare of Stratford-upon-Avon, Warwickshire, than is likely to survive in the next four hundred years about any reader of these words.

What we do not have are entire categories of information – Shakespeare's private letters or diaries, drafts and revisions of poems and plays, critical prefaces or essays, commendatory verse for other writers' works, or instructions guiding his fellow actors in their performances, for instance – that we imagine would help us understand and appreciate his surviving writings. For all we know, many such data never existed as written records. Many literary and theatrical critics, not knowing what might once have existed, more or less cheerfully accept the situation; some even make a theoretical virtue of it by claiming that such data are irrelevant to understanding and interpreting the plays and poems.

So, what do we know about William Shakespeare, the man responsible for thirty-seven or perhaps more plays, more than 150 sonnets, two lengthy narrative poems, and some shorter poems?

While many families by the name of Shakespeare (or some variant spelling) can be identified in the English Midlands as far back as the twelfth century, it seems likely that the dramatist's grandfather, Richard, moved to Snitterfield, a town not far from Stratford-upon-Avon, sometime before 1529. In Snitterfield, Richard Shakespeare leased farmland from the very wealthy Robert Arden. By 1552, Richard's son John had moved to a large house on Henley Street in Stratford-upon-Avon, the house that stands today as "The Birthplace." In Stratford, John Shakespeare traded as a glover, dealt in wool, and lent money at interest; he also served in a variety of civic posts, including "High Bailiff," the municipality's equivalent of mayor. In 1557, he married Robert Arden's youngest daughter, Mary. Mary and John had four sons – William was the oldest – and four daughters, of whom only Joan outlived her most celebrated sibling. William was baptized (an event entered in the Stratford parish church records) on April 26, 1564, and it has become customary, without any good factual support, to suppose he was born on April 23, which happens to be the feast day of Saint George, patron saint of England, and is also the date on which he died, in 1616. Shakespeare married Anne Hathaway in 1582, when he was eighteen and she was twenty-six; their first child was born five months later. It has been generally assumed that the marriage was enforced and subsequently unhappy, but these are only assumptions; it has been estimated, for instance, that up to one third of Elizabethan brides were pregnant when they married. Anne and William Shakespeare had three children: Susanna, who married a prominent local physician, John Hall; and the twins Hamnet, who died young in 1596, and Judith, who married Thomas Quiney – apparently a rather shady individual. The name Hamnet was unusual but not unique: he and his twin sister were named for their godparents, Shakespeare's neighbors Hamnet and Judith Sadler. Shakespeare's father died in 1601 (the year of *Hamlet*), and Mary Arden Shakespeare died in 1608 (the year of *Coriolanus*). William Shakespeare's last surviving direct descendant was his granddaughter Elizabeth Hall, who died in 1670.

Between the birth of the twins in 1585 and a clear reference to Shakespeare as a practicing London dramatist in Robert Greene's sensationalizing, satiric pamphlet, *Greene's Groatsworth of Wit* (1592), there is no record of where William Shakespeare was or what he was doing. These seven so-called lost years have been imaginatively filled by scholars and other students of Shakespeare: some think he traveled to Italy, or fought in the Low Countries, or studied law or medicine, or worked as an apprentice actor/writer, and so on to even more fanciful possibilities. Whatever the biographical facts for those "lost" years, Greene's nasty remarks in 1592 testify to professional envy and to the fact that Shakespeare already had a successful career in London. Speaking to his fellow playwrights, Greene warns both generally and specifically:

> . . . trust them [actors] not: for there is an upstart crow, beautified with our feathers, that with his tiger's heart wrapped in a player's hide supposes he is as well able to bombast out a blank verse as the best of you; and being an absolute Johannes Factotum, is in his own conceit the only Shake-scene in a country.

The passage mimics a line from *3 Henry VI* (hence the play must have been performed before Greene wrote) and seems to say that "Shake-scene" is both actor and playwright, a jack-of-all-trades. That same year, Henry Chettle protested Greene's remarks in *Kind-Heart's Dream,* and each of the next two years saw the publication of poems – *Venus and Adonis* and *The Rape of Lucrece,* respectively – publicly ascribed to (and dedicated by) Shakespeare. Early in 1595 he was named one of the senior members of a prominent acting company, the Lord Chamberlain's Men, when they received payment for court performances during the 1594 Christmas season.

Clearly, Shakespeare had achieved both success and reputation in London. In 1596, upon Shakespeare's application, the College of Arms granted his father the now-familiar coat of arms he had taken the first steps to obtain almost twenty years before, and in 1598, John's son – now permitted to call himself "gentleman" – took a 10 percent share in the new Globe playhouse. In 1597, he bought a substantial bourgeois house, called New Place, in Stratford – the garden remains, but Shakespeare's house, several times rebuilt, was torn down in 1759 – and over the next few years Shakespeare spent large sums buying land and making other investments in the town and its environs. Though he worked in London, his family remained in Stratford, and he seems always to have considered Stratford the home he would eventually return to. Something approaching a disinterested appreciation of Shakespeare's popular and professional status appears in Francis Meres's *Palladis Tamia* (1598), a not especially imaginative and perhaps therefore persuasive record of literary reputations. Reviewing contemporary English writers, Meres lists the titles of many of Shakespeare's plays, including one not now known, *Love's Labor's Won*, and praises his "mellifluous & hony-tongued" "sugred Sonnets," which were then circulating in manuscript (they were first collected in 1609). Meres describes Shakespeare as "one of the best" English playwrights of both comedy and tragedy. In *Remains . . . Concerning Britain* (1605), William Camden – a more authoritative source than the imitative Meres – calls Shakespeare one of the "most pregnant witts of these our times" and joins him with such writers as Chapman, Daniel, Jonson, Marston, and Spenser. During the first decades of the seventeenth century, publishers began to attribute numerous play quartos, including some non-Shakespearean ones, to Shakespeare, either by name or initials, and we may assume that they deemed Shakespeare's name and supposed authorship, true or false, commercially attractive.

For the next ten years or so, various records show

Shakespeare's dual career as playwright and man of the theater in London, and as an important local figure in Stratford. In 1608-9 his acting company – designated the "King's Men" soon after King James had succeeded Queen Elizabeth in 1603 – rented, refurbished, and opened a small interior playing space, the Blackfriars theater, in London, and Shakespeare was once again listed as a substantial sharer in the group of proprietors of the playhouse. By May 11, 1612, however, he describes himself as a Stratford resident in a London lawsuit – an indication that he had withdrawn from day-to-day professional activity and returned to the town where he had always had his main financial interests. When Shakespeare bought a substantial residential building in London, the Blackfriars Gatehouse, close to the theater of the same name, on March 10, 1613, he is recorded as William Shakespeare "of Stratford upon Avon in the county of Warwick, gentleman," and he named several London residents as the building's trustees. Still, he continued to participate in theatrical activity: when the new Earl of Rutland needed an allegorical design to bear as a shield, or *impresa,* at the celebration of King James's Accession Day, March 24, 1613, the earl's accountant recorded a payment of 44 shillings to Shakespeare for the device with its motto.

For the last few years of his life, Shakespeare evidently concentrated his activities in the town of his birth. Most of the final records concern business transactions in Stratford, ending with the notation of his death on April 23, 1616, and burial in Holy Trinity Church, Stratford-upon-Avon.

THE QUESTION OF AUTHORSHIP

The history of ascribing Shakespeare's plays (the poems do not come up so often) to someone else began, as it continues, peculiarly. The earliest published claim that someone else wrote Shakespeare's plays appeared in an 1856 article by Delia Bacon in the American journal *Putnam's Monthly* – although an Englishman, Thomas Wilmot, had shared his doubts in private (even secretive) conversations with friends near the end of the eighteenth century. Bacon's was a sad personal history that ended in madness and poverty, but the year after her article, she published, with great difficulty and the bemused assistance of Nathaniel Hawthorne (then United States Consul in Liverpool, England), her *Philosophy of the Plays of Shakspere Unfolded.* This huge, ornately written, confusing farrago is almost unreadable; sometimes its intents, to say nothing of its arguments, disappear entirely beneath near-raving, ecstatic writing. Tumbled in with much supposed "philosophy" appear the claims that Francis Bacon (from whom Delia Bacon eventually claimed descent), Walter Ralegh, and several other contemporaries of Shakespeare's had written the plays. The book had little impact except as a ridiculed curiosity.

Once proposed, however, the issue gained momentum among people whose conviction was the greater in proportion to their ignorance of sixteenth- and seventeenth-century English literature, history, and society. Another American amateur, Catherine P. Ashmead Windle, made the next influential contribution to the cause when she published *Report to the British Museum* (1882), wherein she promised to open "the Cipher of Francis Bacon," though what she mostly offers, in the words of S. Schoenbaum, is "demented allegorizing." An entire new cottage industry grew from Windle's suggestion that the texts contain hidden, cryptographically discoverable ciphers – "clues" – to their authorship; and today there are not only books devoted to the putative ciphers, but also pamphlets, journals, and newsletters.

Although Baconians have led the pack of those seeking a substitute Shakespeare, in *"Shakespeare" Identified* (1920), J. Thomas Looney became the first published

"Oxfordian" when he proposed Edward de Vere, seventeenth earl of Oxford, as the secret author of Shakespeare's plays. Also for Oxford and his "authorship" there are today dedicated societies, articles, journals, and books. Less popular candidates – Queen Elizabeth and Christopher Marlowe among them – have had adherents, but the movement seems to have divided into two main contending factions, Baconian and Oxfordian. (For further details on all the candidates for "Shakespeare," see S. Schoenbaum, *Shakespeare's Lives,* 2nd ed., 1991.)

The Baconians, the Oxfordians, and supporters of other candidates have one trait in common – they are snobs. Every pro-Bacon or pro-Oxford tract sooner or later claims that the historical William Shakespeare of Stratford-upon-Avon could not have written the plays because he could not have had the training, the university education, the experience, and indeed the imagination or background their author supposedly possessed. Only a learned genius like Bacon or an aristocrat like Oxford could have written such fine plays. (As it happens, lucky male children of the middle class had access to better education than most aristocrats in Elizabethan England – and Oxford was not particularly well educated.) Shakespeare received in the Stratford grammar school a formal education that would daunt many college graduates today; and popular rival playwrights such as the very learned Ben Jonson and George Chapman, both of whom also lacked university training, achieved great artistic success, without being taken as Bacon or Oxford.

Besides snobbery, one other quality characterizes the authorship controversy: lack of evidence. A great deal of testimony from Shakespeare's time shows that Shakespeare wrote Shakespeare's plays and that his contemporaries recognized them as distinctive and distinctly superior. (Some of that contemporary evidence is collected in E. K. Chambers, *William Shakespeare: A Study of Facts and Problems,* 2 vols., 1930.) Since that testimony comes from Shakespeare's enemies and theatrical competitors as well as from his co-workers and from the Elizabethan equivalent of literary journalists, it seems unlikely that, if any of these sources had known he was a fraud, they would have failed to record that fact.

Books About Shakespeare's Theater

Useful scholarly studies of theatrical life in Shakespeare's day include: G. E. Bentley, *The Jacobean and Caroline Stage,* 7 vols. (1941-68), and the same author's *The Professions of Dramatist and Player in Shakespeare's Time, 1590-1642* (1986); E. K. Chambers, *The Elizabethan Stage,* 4 vols. (1923); R. A. Foakes, *Illustrations of the English Stage, 1580-1642* (1985); Andrew Gurr, *The Shakespearean Stage,* 3rd ed. (1992), and the same author's *Play-going in Shakespeare's London,* 2nd ed. (1996); Edwin Nungezer, *A Dictionary of Actors* (1929); Carol Chillington Rutter, ed., *Documents of the Rose Playhouse* (1984).

Books About Shakespeare's Life

The following books provide scholarly, documented accounts of Shakespeare's life: G. E. Bentley, *Shakespeare: A Biographical Handbook* (1961); E. K. Chambers, *William Shakespeare: A Study of Facts and Problems,* 2 vols. (1930); S. Schoenbaum, *William Shakespeare: A Compact Documentary Life* (1977); and *Shakespeare's Lives,* 2nd ed. (1991), by the same author. Many scholarly editions of Shakespeare's complete works print brief compilations of essential dates and events. References to Shakespeare's works up to 1700 are collected in C. M. Ingleby et al., *The Shakespeare Allusion-Book,* rev. ed., 2 vols. (1932).

The Texts of Shakespeare

As FAR AS WE KNOW, only one manuscript conceivably in Shakespeare's own hand may (and even this is much disputed) exist: a few pages of a play called *Sir Thomas More,* which apparently was never performed. What we do have, as later readers, performers, scholars, students, are printed texts. The earliest of these survive in two forms: quartos and folios. Quartos (from the Latin for "four") are small books, printed on sheets of paper that were then folded in fours, to make eight double-sided pages. When these were bound together, the result was a squarish, eminently portable volume that sold for the relatively small sum of sixpence (translating in modern terms to about $5.00). In folios, on the other hand, the sheets are folded only once, in half, producing large, impressive volumes taller than they are wide. This was the format for important works of philosophy, science, theology, and literature (the major precedent for a folio Shakespeare was Ben Jonson's *Works,* 1616). The decision to print the works of a popular playwright in folio is an indication of how far up on the social scale the theatrical profession had come during Shakespeare's lifetime. The Shakespeare folio was an expensive book, selling for between fifteen and eighteen shillings, depending on the binding (in modern terms, from about $150 to $180). Twenty Shakespeare plays of the thirty-seven that survive first appeared in quarto, seventeen of which appeared during Shakespeare's lifetime; the rest of the plays are found only in folio.

The First Folio was published in 1623, seven years after Shakespeare's death, and was authorized by his fellow actors, the co-owners of the King's Men. This publication was certainly a mark of the company's enormous respect for Shakespeare; but it was also a way of turning the old plays, most of which were no longer current in the play-house, into ready money (the folio includes only Shakespeare's plays, not his sonnets or other nondramatic verse). Whatever the motives behind the publication of the folio, the texts it preserves constitute the basis for almost all later editions of the playwright's works. The texts, however, differ from those of the earlier quartos, sometimes in minor respects but often significantly – most strikingly in the two texts of *King Lear,* but also in important ways in *Hamlet, Othello,* and *Troilus and Cressida.* (The variants are recorded in the textual notes to each play in the new Pelican series.) The differences in these texts represent, in a sense, the essence of theater: the texts of plays were initially not intended for publication. They were scripts, designed for the actors to perform – the principal life of the play at this period was in performance. And it follows that in Shakespeare's theater the playwright typically had no say either in how his play was performed or in the disposition of his text – he was an employee of the company. The authoritative figures in the theatrical enterprise were the shareholders in the company, who were for the most part the major actors. They decided what plays were to be done; they hired the playwright and often gave him an outline of the play they wanted him to write. Often, too, the play was a collaboration: the company would retain a group of writers, and parcel out the scenes among them. The resulting script was then the property of the company, and the actors would revise it as they saw fit during the course of putting it on stage. The resulting text belonged to the company. The playwright had no rights in it once he had been paid. (This system survives largely intact in the movie industry, and most of the playwrights of Shakespeare's time were as anonymous as most screenwriters are today.) The script could also, of course, continue to change as the tastes of audiences and the requirements of the actors changed. Many – perhaps most – plays were revised when they were reintroduced after any substantial absence from the repertory, or when they were performed by a company different from the one that originally commissioned the play.

Shakespeare was an exceptional figure in this world because he was not only a shareholder and actor in his company, but also its leading playwright – he was literally his own boss. He had, moreover, little interest in the publication of his plays, and even those that appeared during his lifetime with the authorization of the company show no signs of any editorial concern on the part of the author. Theater was, for Shakespeare, a fluid and supremely responsive medium – the very opposite of the great classic canonical text that has embodied his works since 1623.

The very fluidity of the original texts, however, has meant that Shakespeare has always had to be edited. Here is an example of how problematic the editorial project inevitably is, a passage from the most famous speech in *Romeo and Juliet,* Juliet's balcony soliloquy beginning "O Romeo, Romeo, wherefore art thou Romeo?" Since the eighteenth century, the standard modern text has read,

> What's Montague? It is nor hand, nor foot,
> Nor arm, nor face, nor any other part
> Belonging to a man. O be some other name!
> What's in a name? That which we call a rose
> By any other name would smell as sweet.
>   (II.2.40-44)

Editors have three early texts of this play to work from, two quarto texts and the folio. Here is how the First Quarto (1597) reads:

> Whats *Mountague?* It is nor hand nor foote,
> Nor arme, nor face, nor any other part.
> Whats in a name? That which we call a Rofe,
> By any other name would fmell as fweet:

Here is the Second Quarto (1599):

> Whats *Mountague*? it is nor hand nor foote,
> Nor arme nor face, ô be some other name
> Belonging to a man.
> Whats in a name that which we call a rose,
> By any other word would smell as sweete,

And here is the First Folio (1623):

> What's *Mountague*? it is nor hand nor foote,
> Nor arme, nor face, O be some other name
> Belonging to a man.
> What? in a names that which we call a Rose,
> By any other word would smell as sweete,

There is in fact no early text that reads as our modern text does – and this is the most famous speech in the play. Instead, we have three quite different texts, all of which are clearly some version of the same speech, but none of which seems to us a final or satisfactory version. The transcendently beautiful passage in modern editions is an editorial invention: editors have succeeded in conflating and revising the three versions into something we recognize as great poetry. Is this what Shakespeare "really" wrote? Who can say? What we can say is that Shakespeare always had performance, not a book, in mind.

Books About the Shakespeare Texts

The standard study of the printing history of the First Folio is W. W. Greg, *The Shakespeare First Folio* (1955). J. K. Walton, *The Quarto Copy for the First Folio of Shakespeare* (1971), is a useful survey of the relation of the quartos to the folio. The second edition of Charlton Hinman's *Norton Facsimile* of the First Folio (1996), with a new introduction by Peter Blayney, is indispensable. Stanley Wells, Gary Taylor, John Jowett, and William Montgomery, *William Shakespeare: A Textual Companion*, keyed to the Oxford text, gives a comprehensive survey of the editorial situation for all the plays and poems.

THE GENERAL EDITORS

Introduction

"ALL THE ARGUMENT is a whore and a cuckold." In this single, pungent sentence from *Troilus and Cressida* (II.3.71–72), Shakespeare's Thersites boils down the great events of the Trojan War to farce. For Thersites, the romantic Helen of Troy, whose face, according to Shakespeare's contemporary Christopher Marlowe, had "launched a thousand ships" (*Dr. Faustus,* l. 1328), is just another unfaithful wife, quarreling with her cuckolded husband, Menelaus. In Thersites' jaundiced view, the great events and personalities of Homer's *Iliad,* the founding epic of all Western literature, lose their sublimity and world-historical importance. In essence, the Trojan War is nothing but a sordid, age-old marital quarrel into which others have been drawn; it is the stuff of comedy, not epic.

Although Thersites does not speak for Shakespeare, his comment resonates in a play in which Homer's epic is subjected to unusually intense critical scrutiny. Homer's story of the Trojan War may have seemed both imaginatively gripping and culturally inescapable to Shakespeare, as it did to most of his educated contemporaries, yet Shakespeare's selective retelling of the story in *Troilus and Cressida* does little to uphold the epic grandeur of its original. For Shakespeare, unlike his contemporary George Chapman, who translated Homer into English, the legacy of the *Iliad* appears to have been more dubious than inspiring. *Troilus and Cressida* questions the heroic legend of the Trojan War and strips its leading characters (Hector, Achilles, Agamemnon, Ulysses, and Aeneas, among others) of their legendary charisma, revealing an often shameful although humanly recognizable underlying reality. Shakespeare particularly questions whether the opposed parties to the war represent opposing civilizations, on whose respective victory or defeat the future of the world depends. In the play, the Trojan War often seems more like a male power struggle in a very large aristocratic family than like a clash of cultural opposites; bonds of kinship and courtship cross the battle lines. The nameless rank and file seems merely expendable. When Pandarus dismisses the common soldiers as "chaff and bran" (I.2.236), he speaks for an attitude of lordly contempt that the play does little to contradict.

Not just the narratives but the very language of epic comes under sharp scrutiny in *Troilus and Cressida*, all the more so (or all the more necessarily so) because of their enduring appeal. Since, as far as we know, Shakespeare could not have read Homer in Greek, he relied on other sources both for the narrative of the Trojan War and for his models of epic diction. While various Elizabethan writers, including Christopher Marlowe, had been attempting to fashion a heroic, elevated style for English poetry and drama, George Chapman's 1598 translation of Homer provided the leading model for English epic diction at the time Shakespeare was writing *Troilus and Cressida*. Shakespeare echoes and parodies the gorgeous yet grandiose, polysyllabic, circumlocutory language of English epic-in-translation in the prologue and many of the speeches in *Troilus and Cressida*. That prologue promises epic action, yet the promise is frustratingly belied by the paralysis manifest in the play's opening scenes. Debate about why the war seems to have bogged down replaces action, and, in these verbal exchanges, grandiloquent language appears to be less the language of a heroic age or of epic narrative than of the aging leaders on both sides of the Trojan War. Priam, Agamemnon, and Nestor conceive of themselves as superhuman living legends, yet their pompous, unwieldy eloquence at once belies their power and betrays their impotence. Members of the play's younger generation, who do not think of themselves as characters in an epic, tend to speak differently, in registers varying from political calculation through cynicism to surly contempt and sour disaffection (the principal exception is the incipient epic hero Aeneas). For Troilus, the idealist of the younger generation, elevation belongs more authentically to the personal language of romance than the public one of epic. Early in the play Troilus vents his private disgust about the war:

> Fools on both sides! Helen must needs be fair,
> When with your blood you daily paint her thus.
> I cannot fight upon this argument.
>
> (I.1.89-91)

The "argument" of his own love is more inspiring to him.

A strong impulse of skeptical exposure is thus present in *Troilus and Cressida*. The play even allows us to witness the birth of a legend. We see the Greek Achilles ordering his followers, the Myrmidons, to surround Hector, the leading Trojan warrior, on the battlefield and slaughter him. Achilles instructs them then to spread the story that he alone conquered Hector. That is what happens when Achilles and the Myrmidons kill the disarmed Hector on the battlefield, and that, as Shakespeare suggests, is how heroic legends of individual prowess are born. This episode among others gives an edge to Thersites' taunt to Achilles that he is the "idol of idiot-worshipers" (V.1.7).

It may seem surprising to us that Shakespeare, living in a different and, we tend to believe, less disillusioned era than our own, sees through the heroics of the Trojan War. We tend to think of the twentieth century (now barely over) as a time of unprecedented historical disillusionment. Repeated, searing experiences of military catastrophe, genocide, political corruption, abusive sexual and racial politics, and collapsing ideals have resulted in forms of disbelief that have often been regarded as belonging peculiarly to the twentieth century. Yet Shakespeare's play demystifies the Trojan War with a critical energy that the twentieth century barely equaled. Indeed, it is for that very reason that *Troilus and Cressida* came into its own only recently. Seldom performed or discussed from the time it was written until the twentieth century, *Troilus and Cressida* became one of the most actively discussed and frequently performed Shakespeare plays. How then, we might ask, did Shakespeare come to write his seemingly anomalous "twentieth-century" play in 1603, the year in which *Troilus and Cressida* was entered in the Stationers' Register?

The first thing to be said is that *Troilus and Cressida* was not as anomalous at the time of writing as it may now seem. Historical scholars have connected Shakespeare's writing of the play to a variety of contemporary circumstances. These include a disillusioned turning against earlier chivalric ideals and military heroism in the last days of Elizabeth I's reign (the queen died in 1603). One specific source of disillusionment was the fall of the Earl of Essex, a powerful favorite of the queen but a military failure whose life ended on the block in 1601 after he made an abortive attempt to incite armed revolt against the queen's ministers. During the period of his ascendancy, Essex had become a complex figure in English literary and cultural representation. On one hand, he could be seen by an author like Edmund Spenser as one more embodiment of the chivalric code and military heroism extolled at the high point of Elizabeth I's rule. He is also the subject of what scholars have regarded as the one indubitable reference to contemporary high politics in Shakespeare: the chorus to Act 5 of *Henry V* includes a passage that reads, "Were now the general of our gracious empress . . . from Ireland coming, / Bringing rebellion broachèd on his sword, / How many would the peaceful city quit / To welcome him!" (V, Chorus, 30-34). On the other hand, as David Bevington has discussed extensively in his introduction to the Arden edition of *Troilus and Cressida,* writers, including George Chapman, identified Essex with the Greek Achilles as a formidable but untrustworthy figure. To the extent that Essex could stand for both the romantic chivalry and the dark violence that Shakespeare projects as, respectively, "Trojan" and "Greek" in *Troilus and Cressida*, he already figured a national "identity crisis" in the making. The turbulent and not always courteous Essex helped make visible just how acutely problematic the high Elizabethan code of chivalry and military heroism had become by the end of the 1590s. Also rendered questionable were the poetic genres of epic and romance (often blended, with crisscrossing metaphors, in the long, heroic poems of the Renaissance), on which so much Elizabethan cultural and political life had been modeled. Edmund Spenser's *The Faerie Queene* (1590, 1596) was the exemplary "epic romance" of the Elizabethan period, and life followed art as the queen's favorites vied with one another for military glory and her regard.

Moreover, in the English national mythology widely promulgated during Elizabeth's reign, Britain was supposed to have been founded by a descendant of Aeneas, the Trojan hero who, in Virgil's *Aeneid*, escaped the fall of Troy to found a new Trojan civilization on Italian soil. Appropriating this story in the national interest, English writers, including Spenser, called London "Troynovant," the new Troy. These writers thus laid claim on behalf of England to an epic history and an imperial destiny. Shakespeare reveals a certain skepticism about the grandiose vision and language of this history in plays other than *Troilus and Cressida*, the near-contemporary *Hamlet* (published 1603) being one of them. Yet in *Troilus and Cressida*, skepticism moves closer to outright dismissal than it does anywhere else in his work. Shakespeare returns to the very origins of this history in the narrative of the Trojan War, emphasizing both the doom that faces Troy and the bankruptcy of the honor for which Troy is fighting.

When, for example, the Trojan warrior Hector challenges any Greek champion to meet him in single combat to defend their respective ladies' honor, he is acting out the popular Elizabethan script of romantic chivalry. The fact that Hector's "lady" presumably isn't his wife, Andromache, underlines the courtly conventionality of the gesture; every courtier serves his ideal lady-love, one often, no doubt, imaginary. Yet his gesture seems jarringly misplaced in a war in which chivalry is evidently becoming a thing of the past. Even the idealistic Troilus chides Hector towards the end of the play for chivalrously sparing the lives of Greeks he has conquered. When Hector replies, "Fie, savage, fie!" Troilus retorts, "Hector, then 'tis wars" (V.3.49).

Hector's murder by the followers of Achilles, and the dragging of his corpse over the battlefield behind Achilles' horse, seemingly brings the epic romance of Troy to a definitive close. Yet its demise is never really in doubt from the moment when Hector, although having argued against the continuation of a war fought in a bad cause, caves in to the demands of Troilus and his supporters that the war continue for the honor of all concerned. Hector, no less than the others, is helplessly imprisoned by Trojan "honor." His better judgment cannot release him or the city of which he is the leading warrior. The younger Greeks predictably deride his challenge to single combat ("'tis trash," says Achilles, II.1.125), even though they try to exploit it for their own political ends. Ulysses and Nestor also tellingly agree that the real object of Hector's challenge is Achilles, such challenges belonging to a world of male bonding and emulous rivalry.

A critique of the Trojans is voiced by various speakers on the Greek side. It is mainly from the Greeks, in fact, that we hear a language of political realism, analysis, and calculation in the play. That language is being spoken even when the Greek arch-plotter Ulysses upholds traditional rank and hierarchy in his famous speech on "degree":

The heavens themselves, the planets, and this center
Observe degree, priority, and place,
Insisture, course, proportion, season, form,
Office, and custom, in all line of order.

(I.3.85–88)

While critics have sometimes regarded Ulysses' magnificent, long speech as the definitive profession of Shakespeare's political faith, Ulysses is in fact advocating subordination in the service of his own political designs. Although he is upholding the authority of Agamemnon as the supreme Greek commander, and producing an image of cosmic order based on obedience to higher law, his view is more a matter of manipulative expediency than faith. He certainly has no intention of sacrificing his own political initiative, nor his intent to be the power behind the scenes on the Greek side. The Greeks, most notably Ulysses, may thus herald a "new" politics – or a new, thoroughly political, consciousness – emerging at the end of Elizabeth I's reign. Some critics have connected that shift to broader trends of the early modern era, including the advent of a Machiavellian political science to replace increasingly outmoded feudal and chivalric conceptions inherited from the European Middle Ages. Yet even if this supposition is correct, it does not follow that the Greeks are vindicated in the play. In the end, the Greek victory has more to do with chance and passion than with anyone's calculations. Greek political realism thus seems scarcely an improvement, prone to its own illusions of control over the unpredictable vagaries of human action.

Ulysses tries to become the power behind the scenes in an unusually literal sense. He uses calculated theatrical means to bring a reluctant Achilles into the action. To arouse Achilles' jealousy, he arranges a performance in which the Greeks will pretend to admire Ajax (whom they despise) as a hero and disdain Achilles. Ulysses is thus, in effect, scripting those around him as puppets in his own political play, thereby seeking a control over human affairs akin to that of a playwright. What brings Achilles into the action, however, is not Ulysses' stratagem but the hero's rage at the battlefield death of his friend and bedfellow Patroclus, contemptuously described by Thersites as Achilles' "masculine whore" (V.1.17). The one certainty appears to be uncertainty, and the gap between wishes and outcomes – or, in fact, between anyone's language and the reality it attempts to bring into being – remains ironically wide throughout the play. Traditional English attachment to the Trojan cause and fantasies of a Trojan rebirth on English soil thus take a severe beating in *Troilus and Cressida*. Pandarus, who gets the last word in the play, prophesies something other than ever-expanding imperial glory for England. In his concluding, sardonic vision, colored by his vocation as bawd, he foresees little more than the endless spread of venereal disease through prostitution in England.

The general fading of Elizabethan epic romance, not merely the fate of the troublesome Earl of Essex, probably goes a long way to explain why Shakespeare centers his version of the Trojan War story on the *ill-fated* love affair of Troilus and Cressida. Their story doesn't even appear in Homer's *Iliad*. It was a medieval invention known to Shakespeare mainly from Chaucer's magnificent poem in Middle English called *Troilus and Criseyde*. Although Chaucer's story ends badly, many subsequent readers (and English courtier poets) nevertheless found it poignantly romantic, as they did the figure of the faithful, grieving Troilus, betrayed by Criseyde. They could do so partly because of Chaucer's sympathetically restrained presentation of the characters, however flawed. In Shakespeare's version, the lovers by no means forfeit sympathy, yet Shakespeare's retelling of the story seems motivated by a far more unyielding critical impulse than Chaucer's. The voices of satirical commentary are both more diverse and more scathing in the play than they are in Chaucer's poem.

In the play, the lovers are separated just when their love has been consummated. Cressida's father, Calchas, a traitor who has deserted to the Greeks, asks that she be exchanged for the captured Trojan Antenor. Neither Troilus nor Cressida can prevent this exchange. Cressida will be handed over to Diomedes, who will, in fact, become the first of her new "protectors" in the Greek camp. After the separation, neither the lovers nor Pandarus can prevent fate from taking its course, nor can they themselves escape becoming the bywords they have feared they will become. Troilus becomes fixed as the image of the ever-faithful, grieving lover, who witnesses his own betrayal with incredulity in a scene set up by Ulysses (who is proving his own point about women's unworthiness). Cressida becomes fixed as the image of the unfaithful, wanton woman. Pandarus's name becomes synonymous with pimping; he is the prototypical pander. In the play's perspective, then, high romance proves to be accident-prone and thoroughly ill-fated. Yet cross-purposes and suspicions that have been present all along in the lovers' relationship come sharply into view as their love story ends. Ultimately, it has been an ideal romance only in the mind of Troilus, projecting his own male absolutism onto Cressida while contradictorily revealing his fear of betrayal, that fear being inflamed by his own overwrought sensuality. Indeed, the lovers are stereotypically mismatched insofar as they play the respective roles of the idealistic male lover and the realistic female one.

That particular mismatch is evident in other plays by Shakespeare, notably *The Merchant of Venice, Romeo and Juliet,* and *As You Like It,* yet in *Troilus and Cressida* it is cruelly exposed by the circumstances of the war. Moreover, Shakespeare's plotting of this mismatch is affected by its unpropitious setting in *Troilus and Cressida.* Both lovers are realists in offering no resistance to their separation. Indeed, Troilus insists on its necessity, and Cressida acquiesces despite her anguished protestations. They know that their personal will cannot possibly interfere with the impersonal mechanics of the war. The powers of romance are thus severely circumscribed in the play, and the fatalism of both lovers renders ironic Troilus's commitment in the aftermath of the separation to an unchanged love between himself and his idealized Cressida. His idealism does not blind him to the facts of their situation but rather to the consequences that flow from those facts. Cressida, in contrast, reveals a deep, underlying pessimism throughout. At some level of consciousness she knows that their love is doomed and that she *will* betray Troilus: in this play, a single woman will always be at the disposal of whichever male "protector" successfully lays claim to her. Thus when Cressida hesitates momentarily in her love dialogue with Troilus, he asks, "What too-curious dreg espies my sweet lady in the fountain of our love?" She replies, "More dregs than water, if my fears have eyes" (III.2.62-64). She later adds, cryptically, "I have a kind of self resides with you; / But an unkind self, that itself will leave / To be another's fool" (143-45). The very terms in which she pledges her sincere devotion to Troilus are tantamount to an external curse on herself for the betrayal to come: "If I be false or swerve a hair from truth . . . let them say, to stick the heart of falsehood, / 'As false as Cressid'" (179-91).

Critics of the play have tended to blame one or the other lover for the failure of the romance. Cressida's actions all too easily fit the misogynistic stereotype of the treacherous woman, and she has been blamed accordingly. (Her portrayal as a courtesan in the frontispiece to this text represents one deeply entrenched historical view of her.) Recent critics (some of them feminist) have been more inclined to blame Troilus as the male narcissist whose demands on the woman bear little relation to her needs or condition. In fact, Troilus's unquestioning acceptance that Cressida must be traded for Antenor suggests how deeply he is embedded in a system in which women are exchanged, not merely for men but between men. Placing blame on one or the other party may, however, distract attention from the play's critique of romance as such.

The failure is not that of Troilus and Cressida alone, but of Paris and Helen, over whose now-jaded illicit love the entire war is still being fought (pointlessly fought, as many in the play believe). Pandarus vicariously intrudes upon that relationship, too, this time to stoke the dying flames:

Love, love, nothing but love, still love still more!
For, O, love's bow shoots buck and doe.
The shaft confounds not that it wounds,
But tickles still the sore.
(III.1.111-14)

This song, apparently well known to all those present, connects love through a string of puns to the relevant male and female body parts, thus at once titillating and demystifying sexual desire. As shared currency, the song circulates in a sexually knowing community. Pandarus himself thrives by "tickling" jaded as well as inhibited lovers into action; he thus becomes a disconcerting third party to the play's romantic couples – or couplings. By the very fact of trading on the deficiencies of "pure" romance, however, Pandarus exposes those deficiencies. If his presence seems unpleasantly compromising, he can intervene only because romance is already compromised, desire already insufficient.

Troilus and Cressida is unusual for its time in presenting male homosexuality – the relationship between Achilles and Patroclus – as a coexistent "alternative" to heterosexual romance, one in which no compromising go-between seems necessary. There is little doubt about the sexual nature of the relationship. Patroclus himself says to the reluctant Achilles,

Sweet, rouse yourself, and the weak wanton Cupid
Shall from your neck unloose his amorous fold.
(III.3.222-23)

Yet that relationship is presented, in terms probably more Elizabethan than Greek, as inscrutably removed, at least from theatrical view. It transpires mainly in Achilles' tent, to which we are never given direct access. Yet the tent becomes all the more highly charged as a site on account of its inaccessibility, both to us and to interested parties in the play. We hear from the patently resentful Ulysses and

Nestor that in the tent Achilles and Patroclus devise their own theatricals, in which Patroclus parodically assumes the roles of each of the Greek leaders in turn, mocking and deriding all of them. The "threat" represented by this real or imagined subversive theater evidently looms large in the minds of the Greek leaders, possibly because they associate parodic role-playing with homosexuality as the subversive "other" of the play's heterosexually organized world.

These anxieties in the play reflect broader cultural ones of the time, often expressed in Puritan antitheatrical writings, about the alleged close connection between theatrical performance (including cross-dressing) and male homosexuality. Parodic performance of elevated social identities by social inferiors (mainly, professional actors) was also widely regarded as a threat to social order. The open secret of the relationship between Achilles and Patroclus becomes one around which the attitudes and anxieties of characters in the play – but also of readers – tend to display themselves.

As we have seen, Thersites voices one common brand of social contempt in jeering at Patroclus as a masculine whore. Yet even Patroclus feels constrained by the public opprobrium directed at the "effeminate man":

A woman impudent and mannish grown
Is not more loathed than an effeminate man
In time of action. I stand condemned for this.
                                        (III.3.217-19)

Patroclus's consciousness of himself as seen by others reveals one limit to the power he and Achilles share, both to exclude and disable the larger political world. Further limits are revealed by the fact that Achilles is bound in courtship to Polyxena, a daughter of the Trojan king Priam. This situation results in a strange "lover's address" by Achilles to Patroclus about his continuing obligations to Patroclus's female rival:

My sweet Patroclus, I am thwarted quite
From my great purpose in tomorrow's battle.
Here is a letter from Queen Hecuba,
A token from her daughter, my fair love,
Both taxing me and gaging me to keep
An oath that I have sworn.
                                    (V.1.37–42)

It would appear that even the great Achilles is subject to
the public compulsions of heterosexual courtship and
male rivalry over women, and possibly even to crisscrossing trajectories of desire. Furthermore, we unexpectedly
hear from Thersites toward the end of the play that Patroclus is always eager to hear of a "commodious" (V.2.197)
whore. Homosexuality thus does not appear to be an exclusive practice in the play, nor does it appear to confer an
exclusive "identity." In this respect, *Troilus and Cressida*
conforms to what we now believe was the prevailing Elizabethan view. Finally, the clever Ulysses undermines any
sense of absolute autonomy or self-determining singularity
to which Achilles may aspire by persuading him that his
greatness exists only in the view and fickle opinion of others, not within himself. Ulysses warns Achilles that, far
from preserving that greatness in the seclusion of his own
tent, he is forfeiting it:

        The cry went once on thee,
  And still it might, and yet it may again,
  If thou wouldst not entomb thyself alive
  And case thy reputation in thy tent.
                          III.3.183–86)

Ultimately, the death of Patroclus proves this male-male
relationship to be no less vulnerable to the war than any
other. It is through Patroclus's death that Achilles is defin-
itively brought back into the Greek public world he has
both mocked and shunned, but perhaps also rightly
feared.

Troilus and Cressida offers little purchase, then, to romantic idealization of any kind. To the extent that the play promises epic, as it does in its lofty prologue, or romance, as it does in the inception of the relationship between *Troilus and Cressida,* it seems increasingly to deliver comedy and satire instead. The prospect of stirring action gives way anticlimactically to long-winded, pompous talk in the opening scenes, since the war seems to have ground to a halt although its wastefulness continues. Social diversions – and social comedy – fill the dead time of stalemated action. The legendary Greek warrior Ajax, manipulated and scorned by his fellow Greeks, is a comic monster of vanity, convinced of his own modesty; a common Elizabethan joke linked Ajax to A-jakes, meaning a toilet. Grandiose warrior heroism appears to have become nothing more than the fantasy of the play's principal fool. The exceptionally vile, obscene jesting of Thersites and the salacious wit of Pandarus may strike some audiences as disagreeable, yet neither their humor nor their perspective is to be denied. They, among others, make *Troilus and Cressida* a genuinely funny play.

The play's shift of ground from epic romance to comedy and satire follows one of the trends of the moment in which it was written. As the Elizabethan era waned and the carefully stage-managed love affair between the queen and her people drew to an end – a love affair in which, however, Catholics, militant Puritans, and other persecuted minorities were not welcome to participate – public disaffection expressed itself in increasingly vocal although often indirect criticism of the regime. Intensifying social criticism on practically all fronts expressed itself in the proliferating satirical literature of the period, prompting an ecclesiastical ban in 1599 on satires and other writings perceived as socially disruptive. The increased contentiousness of literary production in this period is apparent not just in famous public quarrels like the one between the prose writers Thomas Nashe and Gabriel Harvey, but in the so-called war of the theaters, a highly personal conflict between different playwrights and acting companies, fought onstage in satirical plays of the turn of the century, in which Shakespeare was marginally involved. Scholars have detected many echoes of this other war in *Troilus and Cressida*. The play is very much a product of its milieu and moment.

It is important to emphasize, however, that generic shifts in the course of the play are never complete or one-directional, a fact that has apparently made the play difficult to classify from the start. For the editor of one of the two 1609 quartos, the play was a witty comedy, although it was also billed as a "history" on the title page. In contrast, the compilers of the 1623 folio included the play among the tragedies. Although Shakespeare's plays are all generically mixed, the peculiar resistance of *Troilus and Cressida* to generic classification was increasingly perceived as a critical problem from the nineteenth century onward. It was so partly because the play's diction ranges through so many different registers and partly because a powerful satirical impulse informs the play as a whole.

This generic indeterminacy implies that the sweeping demystification Shakespeare undertakes results in something of a crisis regarding the ability of any inherited literary and cultural forms, or any analytical categories, to make sense of the world. Widely divergent terms, perspectives, and languages embodied in the play fail to come together in any single vision, genre, person, or language. By the time Pandarus becomes the play's only speaker in the concluding epilogue, it is as if all other languages in the play have been exhausted. Even Pandarus's epilogue is one of practically senile impoverishment for all its sardonic wit. Yet this seemingly "terminal" state of affairs does not cancel the complexity or continuing intellectual challenge of *Troilus and Cressida* (an intellectual challenge so marked that critics have speculated that the play was written for a select intellectual audience, such as that of the Inns of Court, where lawyers were trained).

One feature of the play on which modern critics have

seized is its series of brilliantly articulated debates regarding the nature of truth and value. Are these absolute or relative? Based on faith or the evidence of the senses? Fixed or fluctuating? Intrinsic or subject to opinion? Transcendent or market-determined? As exactly those debates became acute in many moments of twentieth-century crisis, critics found themselves drawn back not just to the brilliant formulation of the issues in *Troilus and Cressida* but to their lived reality for the play's characters.

Although not all present-day readers would accept his terms, Troilus experiences his betrayal by Cressida as a crisis of truth itself, not just as a moment of bitter disillusionment. His experiencing it that way reveals something about the wrenching contradictions in which the play is enmeshed. The absolute faith in Cressida to which Troilus has committed himself as a lover – his belief in her enduring "truth" – ultimately comes into direct conflict with the truth he learns by witnessing Cressida betray him. Rather than immediately destroying his faith, this other truth, confirmed by the presence of Ulysses as eyewitness, splits Cressida in Troilus's now-divided mind:

> This she? No, this is Diomed's Cressida.
> If beauty have a soul, this is not she;
> If souls guide vows, if vows be sanctimonies,
> If sanctimony be the gods' delight,
> If there be rule in unity itself,
> This was not she. O madness of discourse,
> That cause sets up with and against itself;
> Bifold authority, where reason can revolt
> Without perdition, and loss assume all reason
> Without revolt. This is and is not Cressid.
>
> (V.2.140–49)

One Cressida is still the object of Troilus's enduring faith, the other the worldly woman who has betrayed him. Faith and knowledge have been placed drastically at odds with each other. The seemingly irrepressible idealizing impulse, of which Troilus is the play's last representative, can finally seize on no object in the world; the true Cressida survives only as a residue or figment in Troilus's fractured mind.

Neither the circumstances of the play nor the character of Troilus allows for a fully tragic development of the conflict between different "truths." A play that moves much closer to full-scale tragedy in this vein is Shakespeare's *Coriolanus,* another play in which the leading character's "truth" (or incorrigible perversity!) is eventually shared by no one in the world around him. Yet both the predicament of Troilus and level of concern in the play about what *does* make sense forestall any characterization of the play as simply "disillusioned" or cynical. That flattening out fails to do justice to the play; so did the tendency of some twentieth-century criticism and performance to overemphasize the sleaze factor, so to speak, at the expense of the play's complex challenge to understanding. What the new century will make of that challenge remains to be seen.

JONATHAN CREWE
Dartmouth College

Note on the Text

TROILUS AND CRESSIDA was published in two versions: first in a quarto edition in 1609, then in the folio volume of Shakespeare's plays in 1623. Two states of the quarto, differing only in their first two pages, were published in 1609. Only one of these states included the publisher's preface that appears in the Pelican text to follow. In the folio, as an apparently late inclusion, the play was printed without being repaginated and without its title appearing in the table of contents. The prologue, included in this edition, appears only in the folio text.

Although the publisher of one version of the 1609 quarto asserts that the play had been performed by "the king's majesties servants at the Globe," the bookseller's preface to the other 1609 version of the quarto somewhat mystifyingly claims that the play had never been performed and was therefore an unblemished offering to the discriminating reader. This preface has contributed to the reputation of *Troilus and Cressida* as an intellectually challenging, sophisticated, bookish play rather than a crowd-pleasing one.

Although the publisher's claim that the play had been performed by the King's Men cannot be discounted (it also does not constitute proof), the bookseller's preface, contradicting that claim, does reflect a turn against the values and pleasures of popular theatrical performance early in the reign of James I. No doubt James's own scholarliness, political authoritarianism, and well-known dislike of being made a public spectacle contributed to this change. By advocating a remote, fastidious exercise of monarchical power, James separated himself from his predecessor, Elizabeth I, who had cultivated popularity and performed spectacularly on the "stage" of her kingdom.

Ben Jonson, Shakespeare's great playwright contemporary, remains notorious to this day for the hostility he displayed toward the public theater even while working in it. His desire to appeal to discriminating readers over the heads of theater audiences resulted in the publication of his plays, under his own editorial control, in the great folio *Works* of 1616. Yet Jonson's stance was not wholly eccentric. Unease and even disgust about pandering to popular taste, as well as a desire to engage intellectually demanding readers, characterize a number of Shakespeare's Jacobean plays from *Hamlet* through *Coriolanus.* Perhaps it isn't wholly coincidental that the pander looms large in *Troilus and Cressida* as a troubling figure. It is by no means clear that Shakespeare would have disapproved of the publisher's appeal to a discriminating readership.

Both critics and textual editors have extensively discussed the different texts and complicated early publication history of the play, some of the peculiarities of which appear to have originated in problems regarding ownership of copyright. Suffice it to note here that both Q and F are fully viable as control texts for any modern edition of the play. Given this fact, I have followed my Pelican predecessor, Virgil Whitaker, in choosing Q, but, in keeping with his own practice and that of most other editors, I have both altered and supplemented Q with materials from F. This editorial practice follows from the generally accepted view that F is directly based on Q. The additions and corrections in F – sometimes thought to have been authorial – generally seem intelligible and they sometimes rectify obvious errors.

All additions or emendations adopted from the folio are listed below, along with other substantive departures from the quarto text. The adopted reading in italics is followed by the quarto reading, if any, in roman (in some cases material lacking in the quarto is simply added from the folio, as noted below). The spelling of "Troilus," "Trojan," and "Cressid(a)" has been regularized throughout. No act and scene divisions appear in Q. The ones included here have been established by previous editors. I have gratefully incorporated much of the work of Virgil Whitaker, and have profited from the work of previous editors and critics, notable among them being David Bevington in his recent, comprehensive F-based edition of the play.

Preface (in Q only) 18 *witted* wittied 32 *judgment's* Iudgements 38 *state* states

Prologue (in F only) 8 *immures* emures 12 *barks* barke 19 *Sperr* Stirre

I.1 25 *of* (F) 26 *you* (F) yea 41 *An* And 53 *Pour'st* (F) Powrest 67 *an* And 70 *travail* trauell 71 *ill-thought-on* (F) ill thought 75 *An* and; *not* (F) 76 *on* (F) a; *care* (F) 77 *an* and 95 *tetchy* teachy; *woo* woe 100 *resides* reides

I.2 1, 2, 12, 15, 19, 33, 37, 39 s.p. ALEXANDER Man 44 *Ilium* (F) Illum 47 *ye* yea 84 *wit* will 114 *lift* (F) liste 123 *an* and 126 *the* thee 136, 147, 149, 151, 154 *hair(s)* heire(s), heare(s) 149 *An't* And t' 186 *shrewd* shrowd 187 *a* (F) 199 *man's* (F) man 204 *anything* anything; *an* and 206 s.d. *Enter Paris* (after 203 in Q) 212 s.d. *Enter Helenus* (after Cressida speaks in Q) 218 *indifferent well.* indifferent, well, 234 s.d. *Enter common Soldiers* (F)

I.3 2 *the* (F) these; *the jaundice on* these Iaundies ore 13 *every* (F) ever 31 *thy* (F) the 36 *patient* (F) ancient 48 *breese* brize 54 *Returns* Retires 56 *spirit* (F) spright 61 *thy* (F) the 72 *lips than* lips; then 70–74 AGAMEMNON *Speak . . . oracle* (F) 75 *basis* (F) bases 87 *Insisture* (F) In sisture 110 *meets* (F) melts 156 *scaffoldage* scoaffollage 157 *o'er-wrested* ore-rested 159 *unsquared* (F) unsquare 179 *natures,* (F) natures 188 *self-willed* (F) selfe-wild 195 *and* (F) our 209 *fineness* (F) finesse 212 s.d. *Tucket* (F) 214 s.d. *Enter Aeneas* (F) 238 *Jove's* (F) great Ioves 247 *affair* (F) affairs 252 *the* (F) that 256 *loud* (F) alowd 262 *this* (F) his 267 *That seeks* (F) And feeds 276 *compass* (F) couple 289 *or means* (F) a meanes 294 *one* (F) no 297 *this withered brawn* (F) my withered braunes 298 *will* (F) 302 *youth* (F) men 304 s.p. AGAMEMNON (F) 305 *first* (F) sir 309 s.d. *Exeunt . . . Nestor* (F) 315 *This 'tis* (F) 327 *Achilles, were* (F) Achilles weare 334 *his honor* (F) those knows 354 *his* in his 354–56 *Which . . . limbs* (F) 369 *we* (F) it 372 *did* (F) do 390 *tarre* (F) arre

II.1 14 *vinewed'st* whinid'st (F) unsalted (Q) 17 *oration* (F) oration without booke 18 *a* (F) 19 *murrain* murrion; *o'* ath 27 *An* and 37 AJAX *Cobloaf!* Aiax Coblofe 38, 40, 41 s.p. THERSITES, AJAX, THERSITES (F) 40 s.d. *Beating him* (F) 45 *Thou* (F) you 54 s.d. *Enter Achilles . . . Patroclus* 70 *I* (F) It 73 *I'll* (F) I 76, 78 s.d. *Ajax threatens . . .* 95 *sufferance* (F) suffrance 100 *if he knock out* (F) and knocke at 104 *your* their; *on their toes* (F) 113 *brach* brooch 121 *fifth* (F) first

II.2 3 *damage* domage 4 *travail* trauell 14, 15 *surety, / Surety* surely, / Surely 17 *worst.* (F) worst 27 *father* (F) fathers 28 *ounces* ounce

33 *at* (F) of   **47** *Let's* (F) Sets   **64** *shores* (F) shore   **67** *chose* (F) choose
79 *stale* (F) pale   **82** *launched* (F) lansh't   **100 s.d.** *Enter Cassandra* after
l. 96 in Q: Enter Cassandra   **179** *benumbèd* benumbed   **182** *refractory*
refracturie   **210** *strike* (F) shrike

II.3   1 s.p. THERSITES (F)   **21 s.d.** *Enter Patroclus* (F)   **25** *wouldst* (F)
couldst   **31** *art* (F) art not; *corse* course   **47** *thyself* (F) Thersites   **55–**
59 PATROCLUS . . . *fool* (F)   **62–63** *of Agamemnon* (F)   **66** *creator* (F)
Prover   **69 s.d.** *Exit* (F)   **73–74** *Now . . . all* (F)   **78** *shent* sent (F) sate
82 *so say* (F) say so   **113** *winged* wingèd   **129** *as* (F) and   **130** *carriage*
of this action (F) streame of his commencement   **140** *enter you* (F) enter-
taine   **159 s.d.** *Enter Ulysses* (after l. 156 in Q)   **191** *titled* (F) liked
200 *armèd* armed   **201** *pash* (F) push   **203** *An* and   **210** *let* (F) tell
213, 217 *An* And   **218 s.p.** ULYSSES (F) Aiax   **219 s.p.** AJAX (F)   **220**
s.p. NESTOR (after *warm* in l. 220 in Q)   **221** *praises* (F) praiers; *pour in,*
pour in (F) poure in, poure   **238** *got* (F) gat   **240** *all* (F) all thy   **246**
bourn (F) boord   **247** *Thy* (F) This   **261** *cull* (F) call

III.1 (bracketed s.d.'s are F)   **6** *noble* (F) notable   **25** *friend* (F)   **35** *you*
not (F) not you   **37** *that* (F)   **89** *poor* (F)   **103** *lord* (F) lad   **110**
In . . . so (F)   **113** *shaft confounds* (F) shafts confound   **144** *these* (F)
this   **152** *thee* (F) her

III.2   3 s.p. BOY Man   **3** *he* (F)   **8** *a* to a   **10** *those* (F) these   **27 s.d.**
Enter Pandarus (F)   **42, 46** *an, An* and   **64** *fears* teares   **76** *is* (F)   **88**
crown it. No perfection (F) lover part no affection   **95 s.d.** *Enter Pandarus*
(F)   **114** *glance that ever–* glance; that ever   **116** *not, till now* (F) till
now not   **128** *Cunning* Comming   **137** *An* and   **152** *might; that*
might, that   **155** *aye* (F) age   **162** *winnowed* winnowèd   **171** *similes*
(F) simele's   **175** *Yet* (F)   **180** *and* (F) or   **188** *as* (F) or   **195** *pains*
(F) paine

III.3   33 *his* this   **39** *to* (F)   **43** *unplausive* (F) vnplausiue   **44** *med'cinable*
medecinable   **100** *shining* (F) aiming   **102** *giver* (F) givers   **119**
formed formèd; *th'* (F) the   **128** *abject* (F) obiect   **140** *on* (F) one   **141**
shrinking (F) shriking   **152** *mail* male   **155** *one* (F) on   **160** *hindmost;*
(F) him, most   **161–63** *Or . . . on* (F)   **162** *rear* neere   **164** *past* (F)
passe   **177** *give* goe   **197** *grain of Pluto's gold* (F) thing   **198** *th'* (F);
deeps (F) depth   **200** *Does* Do   **224** *a* (F)   **233** *we* (F) they   **255** *an*
and   **265** *to him* (F)   **273** *most* (F)   **276–77** *Grecian* (F)   **277** *et*
cetera (F)   **291** *be wi'* buy   **293** *eleven of* a leauen of

IV.1   s.d. *with a torchbearer* with a torch (F)   **4** *you* (F) your   **15** *and, so*
long, and so long   **16** *But* (F) Lul'd   **40–41** *do think* (F) beleeve   **52**
the (F)   **56** *soilure* (F) soyle   **76** *you* (F) they

IV.2   6 *infants'* infants   **22 s.d.** *Enter Pandarus* (F)   **31** *capocchia* chipochia
51 *It's* (F) its   **63** *us* (F); *for him* (F)   **66** *concluded so* (F) so concluded
72 *nature* (F) neighbor Pandar   **77 s.p.** CRESSIDA (F)   **87–88** *I beseech*
you . . . beseech you (F)

IV.4   4 *as* (F) is   **53** *the root* (F) my throate   **63** *there's* (F) there is   **76**
They're . . . nature (F); *They're* Their   **78** *person* (F) portion   **134** *I'll*
(F) I   **138 s.d.** *Sound trumpet* (F)   **143–47** DEIPHOBUS . . . *chivalry* (F)

IV.5   15 *toe* (F) too   **65** *you* (F) the   **73 s.p.** ACHILLES Agamemnon   **95**
s.p. AGAMEMNON (F) Ulisses   **97** *matchless,* (F) matchlesse   **98** *in deeds*

(F) deeds 115 *disposed* (F) dispo'd 131 *Of our rank feud* (F) 132 *drop* (F) day 142 *Oyez* O yes 160 *mine* (F) my 164–69 *But . . . integrity* (F) 177 *that I affect th' untraded oath* (F) thy affect, the untraded earth 187 *thy* (F) th' 192 *hemmed* (F) shrupd 198 *Let* (F) O let 205 *As . . . courtesy* (F) 234 *prithee* (F) pray thee 254 *stithied* (F) stichied 283 *thee* (F) you 286 *As* (F) But 291 *she loved* (F) my Lord

V.1 12 *need these* (F) needs this 13 *boy* (F) box 18-19 *catarrhs* (F) 19 *o'* a 20 *wheezing* whissing 21 *limekilns* lime-kills 23 *and the like* (F) 32 *tassel* (F) toslell 33 *pestered* pestred 38 *in tomorrow's* (F) into morrowes 47 **s.d.** *Exit* (F) 54 *brother* (F) be 56 *hanging* (F); *brother's* (F) bare 58 *farced* (F) faced 59 *he is* (F) her's 60 *dog* (F) day; *mule* (F) Moyle; *fitchew* (F) Fichooke 62 *Menelaus!* Menelaus 63 *not* (F) 77 *sewer* sure 78 *at once* (F) 99 **s.d.** *Exit* Exeunt (F)

V.2 5 **s.d.** *Enter Troilus and Ulysses* (F) 15 **s.p.** CRESSIDA Cal. 36 *you* (F) 40 *Nay* (F) Now 41 *distraction* (F) distruction 46 *withered* witherèd 47 *Why, Greek!* why Greeke? 48 *adieu* (F) 56 *these* (F) 58 *But* (F) 59 *la* lo 67 **s.p.** CRESSIDA (F) Troy: 71 *have't* (F) ha't 77 *in* (F) on 80 **s.p.** DIOMEDES 81 **s.p.** CRESSIDA He 84 **s.p.** CRESSIDA (F) 88 *one's* on's 91 *By* (F) And by 105 *Ay,* (F) I 106 *plagued* (F) plaguèd 116 *say* (F) said 120 *co-act* (F) Court 125 *had deceptious* (F) were deceptions 136 *soil* (F) spoile 154 *orifice* orifex 155 *Ariachne's* (F) Ariachna's 160 *five-* (F) finde 163 *bound* (F) given 170 *as I* I

V.3 14 **s.p.** CASSANDRA (F) Cres. 20–23 **s.p.** *To . . .* CASSANDRA (F) 21 *give* count give; *use* as 29 *mean'st* (F) 85 *distraction* (F) destruction 104 *o' these* ath's

V.4 3 *young* (F) 15 *begin* began 25 *Art thou* (F) art

V.5 22 *scaled* (F) scaling 41 *luck* (F) lust 43 **s.p.** AJAX (F)

V.6 1 **s.p.** AJAX (F) 2 **s.p.** DIOMEDES (F) 13 **s.p.** ACHILLES (F) 13 *see thee* see thee ha 27 *reck* wreake; *thou* (F) I

V.7 1 **s.p.** ACHILLES (F) 10 *'Loo* lowe; *'loo* lowe 11 *horned* hen'd; *'Loo, Paris, 'loo* lowe Paris, lowe 12 **s.d.** *Exeunt* Exit 13, 15, 23 **s.p.** MARGARELON Bastard 16 *am a bastard* (F) am bastard

V.8 4 **s.d.** *his* (F) 15 *part* (F) prat 16 **s.p.** GREEK (F) One 16 *Trojan trumpets* Troyans trumpet

V.9 1 *shout is that* (F) is this

V.10 **s.d.** *and* (F) 3 **s.p.** TROILUS (F) (before l. 2 in Q) 8 *say,* say 12 *fear, of* (F) feare of 17 *there* (F) their 23 *vile* (F) proud 24 *pight* (F) pitcht 29 *frenzy's* (F) frienzes 33 *broker-lackey* broker, lackey; *Ignomy and* (F) ignomyny 50 *your* (F) my

The History of
Troilus and Cressida

[NAMES OF THE ACTORS

PRIAM, *King of Troy*
HECTOR ⎫
TROILUS
PARIS
DEIPHOBUS ⎬ *his sons*
HELENUS
MARGARELON ⎭
CALCHAS, *a Trojan priest, defector to the Greeks*
AENEAS ⎫
ANTENOR ⎬ *Trojan commanders*
PANDARUS, *Cressida's uncle*
CRESSIDA, *Calchas's daughter*
ANDROMACHE, *Hector's wife*
CASSANDRA, *Priam's daughter, a prophetess*
ALEXANDER, *Cressida's servant*
TROILUS'S SERVANT
PARIS'S SERVANT

AGAMEMNON, *the Greek supreme commander*
MENELAUS, *his brother, Helen's husband*
ACHILLES ⎫
AJAX
ULYSSES ⎬ *Greek commanders*
NESTOR
DIOMEDES ⎭
PATROCLUS, *Achilles' companion*
THERSITES, *a scurrilous Greek*
HELEN, *Menelaus's wife and Paris's lover*
DIOMEDES' SERVANT

TROJAN AND GREEK SOLDIERS AND ATTENDANTS

SCENE: *Troy, and the Greek camp before it*]

*

A Never Writer
to an Ever Reader:
News.

Eternal reader, you have here a new play, never staled ¹
with the stage, never clapper-clawed with the palms of ²
the vulgar, and yet passing full of the palm comical; for it ³
is a birth of your brain that never undertook anything ⁴
comical vainly. And were but the vain names of comedies ⁵
changed for the titles of commodities, or of plays for ⁶
pleas, you should see all those grand censors, that now ⁷
style them such vanities, flock to them for the main grace ⁸
of their gravities, especially this author's comedies, that
are so framed to the life that they serve for the most com- ¹⁰
mon commentaries of all the actions of our lives, showing such a dexterity and power of wit that the most
displeased with plays are pleased with his comedies. And
all such dull and heavy-witted worldlings as were never ¹⁴
capable of the wit of a comedy, coming by report of
them to his representations, have found that wit there ¹⁶

Preface (This advertisement was inserted by the publisher – i.e., *a never writer* – in one state of the 1609 quarto edition of *Troilus and Cressida*.) **1** *staled* made stale (by repeated performance) **2–3** *clapper-clawed . . . vulgar* injured by the "claws" of a low, unworthy audience applauding it in performance **3** *passing* surpassingly; *palm comical* comedic excellence (the palm being awarded for outstanding merit) **4** *your brain* i.e., a brain, Shakespeare's in this case **5** *vain* futile, unavailing **6** *commodities* marketable goods **7** *pleas* legal arguments; *grand censors* civic authorities **8–9** *main . . . gravities* compellingly graceful presentation of serious issues **10** *framed . . . life* portrayed true to life **10–11** *common* generally applicable **14** *worldlings* people mired in low, worldly concerns **16** *representations* play performances

that they never found in themselves and have parted better witted than they came, feeling an edge of wit set
upon them more than ever they dreamed they had brain
20   to grind it on. So much and such savored salt of wit is in
his comedies that they seem, for their height of pleasure,
22   to be born in that sea that brought forth Venus.
Amongst all there is none more witty than this, and had
24   I time I would comment upon it, though I know it needs
25   not, for so much as will make you think your testern well
26   bestowed, but for so much worth as even poor I know to
be stuffed in it. It deserves such a labor as well as the best
28   comedy in Terence or Plautus. And believe this, that
29   when he is gone and his comedies out of sale, you will
30   scramble for them and set up a new English Inquisition.
Take this for a warning, and at the peril of your pleasure's
loss, and judgment's, refuse not, nor like this the less for
33   not being sullied with the smoky breath of the multi-
34   tude, but thank fortune for the scape it hath made
35   amongst you, since by the grand possessors' wills I be-
36   lieve you should have prayed for them rather than been
prayed. And so I leave all such to be prayed for, for the
38   state of their wits' healths, that will not praise it. *Vale.*

---

22 *Venus* Roman goddess of love, identified with her Greek counterpart,
Aphrodite, whose name indicates that she was born from sea foam   24–25
needs not is unnecessary   25 *testern* sixpence (the price of a quarto)   26–27
but . . . in it i.e., even to the extent that someone as limited as I can appreciate its merit   28 *Terence, Plautus* celebrated Roman authors of comedy   29
out of sale no longer on the market   30 *English Inquisition* i.e., exhaustive
search, with allusion to the Catholic Inquisition's relentless ferreting out of
heretical documents and meanings   33 *smoky* vaporous, reeking   34–35
scape . . . you i.e., its lucky "escape" into print among you   35 *grand possessors* owners of the title to the play, possibly the King's Men, the acting company to which Shakespeare belonged   36–37 *been prayed* i.e., been invited
to buy   38 *Vale* farewell (Latin)

The History of
Troilus and Cressida

∾ The Prologue

[Spoken by a man in armor.]
[In Troy there lies the scene. From isles of Greece
The princes orgulous, their high blood chafed,   2
Have to the port of Athens sent their ships
Fraught with the ministers and instruments   4
Of cruel war. Sixty and nine, that wore
Their crownets regal, from th' Athenian bay   6
Put forth toward Phrygia, and their vow is made   7
To ransack Troy, within whose strong immures   8
The ravished Helen, Menelaus' queen,   9
With wanton Paris sleeps, and that's the quarrel.   10
To Tenedos they come,   11
And the deep-drawing barks do there disgorge   12
Their warlike fraughtage. Now on Dardan plains   13
The fresh and yet unbruisèd Greeks do pitch
Their brave pavilions. Priam's six-gated city,   15
Dardan, and Timbria, Helias, Chetas, Troien,   16
And Antenonidus, with massy staples   17

Prologue 2 *orgulous* proud; *high blood chafed* i.e., aristocratic spirits aroused **4** *Fraught* laden; *ministers* agents (i.e., soldiers) **6** *crownets* coronets **7** *Phrygia* western Asia Minor **8** *immures* walls **9** *ravished* abducted **10** *quarrel* cause of conflict, complaint **11** *Tenedos* an island close to Troy **12** *deep-drawing barks* heavily laden ships **13** *fraughtage* freight; *Dardan* Trojan, named for Dardanus, a mythical ancestor of the Trojan ruling family **15** *brave pavilions* gorgeous tents; *Priam* king of Troy **16–17** *Dardan . . . Antenonidus* (names of the six gates into the city) **17** *massy staples* large receptacles for bolts

18   And corresponsive and fulfilling bolts,
19   Sperr up the sons of Troy.
20   Now expectation, tickling skittish spirits,
     On one and other side, Trojan and Greek,
22   Sets all on hazard. And hither am I come,
23   A Prologue armed, but not in confidence
24   Of author's pen or actor's voice, but suited
     In like conditions as our argument,
     To tell you, fair beholders, that our play
27   Leaps o'er the vaunt and firstlings of those broils,
     Beginning in the middle, starting thence away
29   To what may be digested in a play.
30   Like or find fault; do as your pleasures are;
     Now good or bad, 'tis but the chance of war.]   *[Exit.]*

                              *

∾ **I.1** *Enter Pandarus and Troilus.*

TROILUS
1   Call here my varlet; I'll unarm again.
     Why should I war without the walls of Troy
     That find such cruel battle here within?
     Each Trojan that is master of his heart,
5   Let him to field; Troilus, alas, hath none.
PANDARUS
6   Will this gear ne'er be mended?
TROILUS
     The Greeks are strong, and skillful to their strength,
     Fierce to their skill, and to their fierceness valiant;
     But I am weaker than a woman's tear,

---

18 *corresponsive and fulfilling* matching and snugly fitting   **19** *Sperr up* protectively lock in   **22** *Sets all on hazard* places everything at risk, as in a gambling game   **23** *not in confidence* not relying on   **24–25** *suited . . . argument* costumed in keeping with the (military) theme of the play   **27** *vaunt and firstlings* preliminaries; *broils* quarrels   **29** *digested* encompassed
     I.1 Troy: before Priam's palace   **1** *varlet* servant boy   **5** *none* i.e., no heart (for battle)   **6** *gear* business; *mended* put right (both *gear* and *mended* implying troublesome male sexual apparatus)

Tamer than sleep, fonder than ignorance,   10
Less valiant than the virgin in the night,
And skilless as unpracticed infancy.
PANDARUS   Well, I have told you enough of this. For my
part, I'll not meddle nor make no farther. He that will   14
have a cake out of the wheat must tarry the grinding.   15
TROILUS   Have I not tarried?
PANDARUS   Ay, the grinding; but you must tarry the bolt-   17
ing.
TROILUS   Have I not tarried?
PANDARUS   Ay, the bolting; but you must tarry the leav-   20
ening.
TROILUS   Still have I tarried.
PANDARUS   Ay, to the leavening; but here's yet in the
word "hereafter" the kneading, the making of the cake,
the heating of the oven, and the baking. Nay, you must
stay the cooling too, or you may chance burn your lips.   26
TROILUS
Patience herself, what goddess e'er she be,
Doth lesser blench at suff'rance than I do.   28
At Priam's royal table do I sit,
And when fair Cressid comes into my thoughts –   30
So, traitor, then she comes when she is thence.   31
PANDARUS   Well, she looked yesternight fairer than ever I
saw her look, or any woman else.
TROILUS
I was about to tell thee, when my heart,
As wedgèd with a sigh, would rive in twain,   35
Lest Hector or my father should perceive me:

_____

10 *fonder* more foolish   14 *meddle nor make* have anything more to do with
it   15 *tarry the grinding* wait for the wheat to be ground (also implying a
need for patience before *grinding* sexual intercourse can occur)   17–18 *bolting* sifting (also practically a synonym for "fucking" as Pandarus continues to
spin out the sexual innuendos)   20–21 *leavening* fermentation (possibly
suggesting impregnation)   26 *burn your lips* (possible reference to venereal
infection)   28 *blench* flinch; *suff'rance* endurance   31 *So . . . thence* i.e., he
"betrays" her whenever he is not thinking of her, and/or she "betrays" him by
absenting herself, leaving him tormented by her image (?)   35 *wedgèd* having had a wedge driven in; *rive* split

37 I have, as when the sun doth light a-scorn,
Buried this sigh in wrinkle of a smile;
But sorrow that is couched in seeming gladness
40 Is like that mirth fate turns to sudden sadness.

41 PANDARUS An her hair were not somewhat darker than
Helen's – well, go to – there were no more comparison
between the women. But, for my part, she is my
kinswoman; I would not, as they term it, praise her, but
45 I would somebody had heard her talk yesterday, as I
46 did. I will not dispraise your sister Cassandra's wit,
but –

TROILUS
O Pandarus! I tell thee, Pandarus –
When I do tell thee there my hopes lie drowned,
50 Reply not in how many fathoms deep
They lie indrenched. I tell thee I am mad
In Cressid's love. Thou answer'st she is fair;
Pour'st in the open ulcer of my heart
Her eyes, her hair, her cheek, her gait, her voice;
Handlest in thy discourse, O, that her hand,
In whose comparison all whites are ink,
57 Writing their own reproach; to whose soft seizure
58 The cygnet's down is harsh, and spirit of sense
Hard as the palm of plowman. This thou tell'st me –
60 As true thou tell'st me – when I say I love her,
But, saying thus, instead of oil and balm,
Thou lay'st in every gash that love hath given me
The knife that made it.

PANDARUS I speak no more than truth.

TROILUS Thou dost not speak so much.

PANDARUS Faith, I'll not meddle in it. Let her be as she
is. If she be fair, 'tis the better for her; an she be not, she
68 has the mends in her own hands.

---

37 *a-scorn* grudgingly (?) 41 *An* if 45 *somebody* i.e., Troilus 46 *wit* intelligence, rationality 57 *to . . . soft seizure* in comparison with the gentle grip or tender feel of which 58 *cygnet* newly hatched swan; *spirit of sense* rarefied fluid believed necessary to transmit bodily sensations to the mind 68 *mends* remedy (i.e., cosmetics)

TROILUS   Good Pandarus, how now, Pandarus?

PANDARUS   I have had my labor for my travail; ill-   70
thought-on of her, and ill-thought-on of you; gone between and between, but small thanks for my labor.

TROILUS   What, art thou angry, Pandarus? What, with me?

PANDARUS   Because she's kin to me, therefore she's not so
fair as Helen. An she were not kin to me, she would be
as fair on Friday as Helen is on Sunday. But what care   76
I? I care not an she were a blackamoor; 'tis all one to me.   77

TROILUS   Say I she is not fair?

PANDARUS   I do not care whether you do or no. She's a
fool to stay behind her father. Let her to the Greeks,   80
and so I'll tell her the next time I see her. For my part,
I'll meddle nor make no more i' th' matter.

TROILUS   Pandarus –

PANDARUS   Not I.

TROILUS   Sweet Pandarus –

PANDARUS   Pray you, speak no more to me. I will leave
all as I found it, and there an end.   *Exit.*   87
        Sound alarum.

TROILUS
Peace, you ungracious clamors! Peace, rude sounds!
Fools on both sides! Helen must needs be fair,
When with your blood you daily paint her thus.   90
I cannot fight upon this argument;   91
It is too starved a subject for my sword.   92
But Pandarus – O gods, how do you plague me!
I cannot come to Cressid but by Pandar,
And he's as tetchy to be wooed to woo   95
As she is stubborn, chaste, against all suit.   96
Tell me, Apollo, for thy Daphne's love,   97

---

76 *as fair . . . Sunday* as fair in ordinary clothes as Helen in her Sunday best
77 *blackamoor* black person   80 *father* i.e., Calchas, a seer who anticipated
the Trojan defeat and deserted to the Greeks   87 s.d. *alarum* signal to arms
90 *paint* apply a cosmetic   91 *argument* subject of contention   92 *starved*
deficient, impoverished   95 *tetchy* fretful, capricious   96 *against all suit* re-
buffing all pleas   97 *Apollo* sun god; *Daphne* nymph pursued by Apollo (she
is saved by being turned into a bay tree)

98   What Cressid is, what Pandar, and what we.
     Her bed is India; there she lies, a pearl.
100 Between our Ilium and where she resides
101 Let it be called the wild and wand'ring flood,
     Ourself the merchant, and this sailing Pandar
     Our doubtful hope, our convoy and our bark.
          Alarum. Enter Aeneas.
AENEAS
     How now, Prince Troilus, wherefore not afield?
TROILUS
105 Because not there. This woman's answer sorts,
     For womanish it is to be from thence.
     What news, Aeneas, from the field today?
AENEAS
     That Paris is returnèd home, and hurt.
TROILUS
     By whom, Aeneas?
AENEAS   Troilus, by Menelaus.
TROILUS
110 Let Paris bleed. 'Tis but a scar to scorn;
111 Paris is gored with Menelaus' horn.
          Alarum.
AENEAS
112 Hark what good sport is out of town today!
TROILUS
     Better at home, if "would I might" were "may."
     But to the sport abroad. Are you bound thither?
AENEAS
     In all swift haste.
TROILUS   Come, go we then together.   *Exeunt.*
                         *

──────

98 *we* I   100 *Ilium* (synonym for Troy, but used more narrowly here for
King Priam's palace)   101 *flood* ocean   105 *sorts* is fitting   111 *horn* (sym-
bol of a cuckold, a man whose wife is known to have been unfaithful; Paris
has stolen Helen from Menelaus)   112 *out of town* outside the walls of the
city

❧ **I.2** *Enter Cressida and [Alexander,] her man.*

CRESSIDA
  Who were those went by?
ALEXANDER   Queen Hecuba and Helen.
CRESSIDA
  And whither go they?
ALEXANDER   Up to the eastern tower,
  Whose height commands as subject all the vale,   3
  To see the battle. Hector, whose patience
  Is as a virtue fixed, today was moved.   5
  He chid Andromache, and struck his armorer,   6
  And, like as there were husbandry in war,   7
  Before the sun rose he was harnessed light,   8
  And to the field goes he, where every flower   9
  Did as a prophet weep what it foresaw   10
  In Hector's wrath.
CRESSIDA   What was his cause of anger?
ALEXANDER
  The noise goes, this: there is among the Greeks   12
  A lord of Trojan blood, nephew to Hector;
  They call him Ajax.
CRESSIDA   Good, and what of him?
ALEXANDER
  They say he is a very man per se   15
  And stands alone.
CRESSIDA   So do all men unless they are drunk, sick, or
  have no legs.
ALEXANDER   This man, lady, hath robbed many beasts of
  their particular additions: he is as valiant as the lion, 20
  churlish as the bear, slow as the elephant; a man into   21

I.2 Before Cressida's house   **3** *commands as subject* dominatingly overlooks;
vale low-lying ground   **5** *moved* exasperated   **6** *chid* scolded   **7** *husbandry*
good management   **8** *harnessed* in armor   **9–11** *every . . . wrath* i.e., the
flowers spilling the early-morning dew seemed to weep prophetically at the
destruction to follow from Hector's rage   **12** *noise* rumor   **15** *per se* singular,
unequaled   **20** *particular additions* distinguishing attributes   **21** *churlish*
fierce, rough

22 whom nature hath so crowded humors that his valor is
23 crushed into folly, his folly sauced with discretion.
There is no man hath a virtue that he hath not a
25 glimpse of, nor any man an attaint but he carries some
stain of it. He is melancholy without cause and merry
27 against the hair. He hath the joints of everything, but
28 everything so out of joint that he is a gouty Briareus,
29 many hands and no use, or purblind Argus, all eyes and
30 no sight.

CRESSIDA   But how should this man that makes me smile
make Hector angry?

33 ALEXANDER   They say he yesterday coped Hector in the
battle and struck him down, the disdain and shame
whereof hath ever since kept Hector fasting and waking.

    [Enter Pandarus.]

CRESSIDA   Who comes here?

ALEXANDER   Madam, your uncle Pandarus.

CRESSIDA   Hector's a gallant man.

ALEXANDER   As may be in the world, lady.

40 PANDARUS   What's that? What's that?

CRESSIDA   Good morrow, uncle Pandarus.

42 PANDARUS   Good morrow, cousin Cressid. What do you
talk of? – Good morrow, Alexander. – How do you,
cousin? When were you at Ilium?

CRESSIDA   This morning, uncle.

PANDARUS   What were you talking of when I came? Was
Hector armed and gone ere ye came to Ilium? Helen
was not up, was she?

CRESSIDA   Hector was gone, but Helen was not up.

50 PANDARUS   E'en so, Hector was stirring early.

CRESSIDA   That were we talking of, and of his anger.

---

22 *humors* qualities of temperament (believed to originate in four bodily fluids, or *humors*)   23 *sauced* seasoned   25 *glimpse* trace; *attaint* stain, blemish   27 *against the hair* perversely, against the natural order of things; *joints* portions   28 *Briareus* mythological giant with a hundred hands   29 *purblind* wholly blind; *Argus* mythological herdsman with eyes all over his body   33 *coped* came to blows with   42 *cousin* niece

PANDARUS   Was he angry?

CRESSIDA   So he says here.

PANDARUS   True, he was so. I know the cause too. He'll lay about him today, I can tell them that; and there's Troilus will not come far behind him. Let them take heed of Troilus, I can tell them that too.

CRESSIDA   What, is he angry too?

PANDARUS   Who, Troilus? Troilus is the better man of the two.   60

CRESSIDA   O Jupiter! there's no comparison.

PANDARUS   What, not between Troilus and Hector? Do you know a man if you see him?

CRESSIDA   Ay, if I ever saw him before and knew him.   64

PANDARUS   Well, I say Troilus is Troilus.

CRESSIDA   Then you say as I say, for I am sure he is not Hector.

PANDARUS   No, nor Hector is not Troilus in some de-   68 grees.

CRESSIDA   'Tis just to each of them; he is himself.   70

PANDARUS   Himself? Alas, poor Troilus, I would he were.   71

CRESSIDA   So he is.

PANDARUS   Condition, I had gone barefoot to India.   73

CRESSIDA   He is not Hector.

PANDARUS   Himself? no, he's not himself. Would a were   75 himself! Well, the gods are above; time must friend or   76 end. Well, Troilus, well, I would my heart were in her body. No, Hector is not a better man than Troilus.

CRESSIDA   Excuse me.   79

PANDARUS   He is elder.   80

CRESSIDA   Pardon me, pardon me.

---

64 *knew him* (with possible implication of knowing him sexually)   **68–69** *in some degrees* "in some respects" or "there's no comparison"   **71** *I would he were* i.e., himself, and not in love   **73** *Condition . . . India* i.e., even if I were to go barefoot to India, he'd hardly be himself   **75** *a* he   **76–77** *time . . . end* time must improve matters or bring them to an end (proverbial)   **79** *Excuse me* I beg to differ

82 PANDARUS Th' other's not come to't; you shall tell me
another tale when th' other's come to't. Hector shall not
84 have his wit this year.
CRESSIDA He shall not need it if he have his own.
PANDARUS Nor his qualities.
87 CRESSIDA No matter.
PANDARUS Nor his beauty.
CRESSIDA 'Twould not become him; his own's better.
90 PANDARUS You have no judgment, niece. Helen herself
91 swore th' other day that Troilus, for a brown favor – for
so 'tis, I must confess – not brown neither –
CRESSIDA No, but brown.
PANDARUS Faith, to say truth, brown and not brown.
CRESSIDA To say the truth, true and not true.
PANDARUS She praised his complexion above Paris.
CRESSIDA Why, Paris hath color enough.
PANDARUS So he has.
CRESSIDA Then Troilus should have too much. If she
100 praised him above, his complexion is higher than his.
He having color enough, and the other higher, is too
102 flaming a praise for a good complexion. I had as lief
Helen's golden tongue had commended Troilus for a
104 copper nose.
PANDARUS I swear to you, I think Helen loves him better
than Paris.
107 CRESSIDA Then she's a merry Greek indeed.
PANDARUS Nay, I am sure she does. She came to him th'
109 other day into the compassed window – and, you know,
110 he has not past three or four hairs on his chin –

---

82 *come to't* come into his full manhood (perhaps implying sexual initiation)
84 *have his wit* equal him in intelligence 87 *No matter* i.e., he doesn't need
them since he has his own 91 *brown favor* dark complexion 102 *flaming*
exaggerated, but also implying an unhealthily florid coloring; *I had as lief* I
would be equally well pleased if 104 *copper nose* (alludes to the use of copper and other metals to make false noses for those whose noses had been
eaten away by syphilis) 107 *merry* (Greeks were proverbially "merry" in
Shakespeare's time; here, Helen is exceptionally light of heart and morals)
109 *compassed window* bay window

CRESSIDA   Indeed, a tapster's arithmetic may soon bring   111
his particulars therein to a total.

PANDARUS   Why, he is very young; and yet will he within
three pound lift as much as his brother Hector.

CRESSIDA   Is he so young a man, and so old a lifter?   115

PANDARUS   But to prove to you that Helen loves him, she
came and puts me her white hand to his cloven chin –   117

CRESSIDA   Juno have mercy, how came it cloven?

PANDARUS   Why, you know 'tis dimpled. I think his smil-
ing becomes him better than any man in all Phrygia.   120

CRESSIDA   O, he smiles valiantly.

PANDARUS   Does he not?

CRESSIDA   O, yes, an 'twere a cloud in autumn.   123

PANDARUS   Why, go to then. But to prove to you that
Helen loves Troilus –

CRESSIDA   Troilus will stand to the proof, if you'll prove   126
it so.

PANDARUS   Troilus? Why, he esteems her no more than I
esteem an addle egg.   129

CRESSIDA   If you love an addle egg as well as you love an   130
idle head, you would eat chickens i' th' shell.

PANDARUS   I cannot choose but laugh to think how she
tickled his chin. Indeed, she has a marvel's white hand,   133
I must needs confess.

CRESSIDA   Without the rack.   135

PANDARUS   And she takes upon her to spy a white hair
on his chin.

CRESSIDA   Alas, poor chin, many a wart is richer.

PANDARUS   But there was such laughing! Queen Hecuba
laughed that her eyes ran o'er –   140

CRESSIDA   With millstones –   141

PANDARUS   And Cassandra laughed.

---

111 *tapster's arithmetic* i.e., the simple addition a bartender can manage
115 *lifter* thief   117 *puts me* puts   123 *an 'twere* as if it were   126 *stand to
the proof* pass the test (implying that he will get an erection)   129 *addle* rotten
133 *marvel's* marvelously   135 *the rack* (1) instrument of torture, (2) being
tortured   141 *millstones* i.e., not tears of real feeling

143 CRESSIDA   But there was a more temperate fire under the
pot of her eyes. Did her eyes run o'er too?

PANDARUS   And Hector laughed.

CRESSIDA   At what was all this laughing?

PANDARUS   Marry, at the white hair that Helen spied on
Troilus' chin.

CRESSIDA   An't had been a green hair, I should have
150 laughed too.

PANDARUS   They laughed not so much at the hair as at
his pretty answer.

CRESSIDA   What was his answer?

PANDARUS   Quoth she, "Here's but two and fifty hairs on
your chin, and one of them is white."

156 CRESSIDA   This is her question.

PANDARUS   That's true; make no question of that. "Two
and fifty hairs," quoth he, "and one white. That white
hair is my father, and all the rest are his sons." "Jupiter!"
160 quoth she, "which of these hairs is Paris, my husband?"
161 "The forked one," quoth he; "pluck't out, and give it
him." But there was such laughing, and Helen so
blushed, and Paris so chafed, and all the rest so
laughed, that it passed.

CRESSIDA   So let it now, for it has been a great while
going by.

PANDARUS   Well, cousin, I told you a thing yesterday.
Think on't.

CRESSIDA   So I do.

170 PANDARUS   I'll be sworn 'tis true. He will weep you, an
171 'twere a man born in April.

172 CRESSIDA   And I'll spring up in his tears, an 'twere a net-
173 tle against May.

Sound a retreat.

143–44 *But . . . eyes* i.e., they didn't boil over like Hecuba's   156 *question* i.e.,
not Troilus's answer   161 *forked* split (representing Menelaus's cuckoldry)
170 *weep you* weep; *an* as if   171–73 *April . . . May* i.e., April showers bring
forth May flowers (proverbial)   172–73 *nettle* i.e., rather than a May
flower – she will be prickly   173 **s.d.** *retreat* trumpet signal for military
forces to withdraw

PANDARUS   Hark, they are coming from the field. Shall
we stand up here and see them as they pass toward
Ilium? Good niece, do; sweet niece, Cressida.

CRESSIDA   At your pleasure.

PANDARUS   Here, here, here's an excellent place; here we
may see most bravely. I'll tell you them all by their   179
names as they pass by, but mark Troilus above the rest.   180
   Enter Aeneas [passing across the stage].

CRESSIDA   Speak not so loud.

PANDARUS   That's Aeneas. Is not that a brave man? He's
one of the flowers of Troy, I can tell you. But mark
Troilus; you shall see anon.
   Enter Antenor [passing across the stage].

CRESSIDA   Who's that?

PANDARUS   That's Antenor. He has a shrewd wit, I can tell
you, and he's a man good enough. He's one o' th' sound-
est judgments in Troy whosoever, and a proper man of   188
person. When comes Troilus? I'll show you Troilus anon.
If he see me, you shall see him nod at me.   190

CRESSIDA   Will he give you the nod?   191

PANDARUS   You shall see.

CRESSIDA   If he do, the rich shall have more.   193
   Enter Hector [passing across the stage].

PANDARUS   That's Hector, that, that, look you, that;
there's a fellow! Go thy way, Hector! There's a brave   195
man, niece. O brave Hector! Look how he looks!
There's a countenance! Is't not a brave man?

CRESSIDA   O, a brave man!

PANDARUS   Is a not? It does a man's heart good. Look you
what hacks are on his helmet. Look you yonder, do you   200
see? Look you there. There's no jesting; there's laying   201
on, take't off who will, as they say. There be hacks!   202

CRESSIDA   Be those with swords?

---

179 *bravely* excellently   188 *proper* good-looking   191 *give you the nod* (1)
give you a nod of recognition, (2) bob his head like a fool   193 *rich . . .
more* i.e., he will add to the folly in which you are already rich   195 *brave* excellent   201–2 *laying on* dealing forceful blows   202 *tak't off who will* let
anyone try to deny it

PANDARUS   Swords, anything, he cares not; an the devil
205   come to him, it's all one. By God's lid, it does one's
heart good.
    Enter Paris [passing across the stage].
Yonder comes Paris, yonder comes Paris. Look ye yonder, niece. Is't not a gallant man too, is't not? Why, this
is brave now. Who said he came hurt home today? He's
210   not hurt. Why, this will do Helen's heart good now, ha?
Would I could see Troilus now. You shall see Troilus
anon.
    Enter Helenus [passing across the stage].
CRESSIDA   Who's that?
PANDARUS   That's Helenus. I marvel where Troilus is.
That's Helenus. I think he went not forth today. That's
Helenus.
217   CRESSIDA   Can Helenus fight, uncle?
218   PANDARUS   Helenus? No. Yes, he'll fight indifferent well.
I marvel where Troilus is. Hark, do you not hear the
220   people cry "Troilus"? Helenus is a priest.
CRESSIDA   What sneaking fellow comes yonder?
    Enter Troilus [passing across the stage].
PANDARUS   Where? Yonder? That's Deiphobus. 'Tis Troilus!
223   There's a man, niece! Hem! Brave Troilus, the prince of
chivalry!
225   CRESSIDA   Peace, for shame, peace!
PANDARUS   Mark him, note him. O brave Troilus! Look
well upon him, niece. Look you how his sword is
bloodied, and his helm more hacked than Hector's; and
how he looks, and how he goes. O admirable youth! he
230   never saw three and twenty. Go thy way, Troilus, go thy
231   way! Had I a sister were a grace, or a daughter a goddess, he should take his choice. O admirable man!

---

205 *lid* eyelid (mild oath, "by God's eyelid")   **217** *Can Helenus fight* i.e.,
since he is a priest   **218** *indifferent* fairly   **223** *Hem* (exclamation, possibly
at having confused Deiphobus with Troilus)   **225** *Peace, for shame* i.e., lower
your voice, don't make fools of us   **231** *grace* i.e., one of three beautiful goddesses in Greek mythology known as the Graces

Paris? Paris is dirt to him; and I warrant Helen, to   233
change, would give an eye to boot.   234

[Enter common Soldiers, passing across the stage.]

CRESSIDA   Here comes more.

PANDARUS   Asses, fools, dolts; chaff and bran, chaff and
bran; porridge after meat. I could live and die in the
eyes of Troilus. Ne'er look, ne'er look. The eagles are
gone; crows and daws, crows and daws. I had rather be   239
such a man as Troilus than Agamemnon and all Greece.   240

CRESSIDA   There is amongst the Greeks Achilles, a better
man than Troilus.

PANDARUS   Achilles? A drayman, a porter, a very camel.   243

CRESSIDA   Well, well.

PANDARUS   "Well, well"? Why, have you any discretion?
Have you any eyes? Do you know what a man is? Is not
birth, beauty, good shape, discourse, manhood, learn-
ing, gentleness, virtue, youth, liberality, and such like,   248
the spice and salt that season a man?

CRESSIDA   Ay, a minced man; and then to be baked with   250
no date in the pie, for then the man's date is out.   251

PANDARUS   You are such a woman a man knows not at   252
what ward you lie.   253

CRESSIDA   Upon my back, to defend my belly; upon my
wit, to defend my wiles; upon my secrecy, to defend   255
mine honesty; my mask, to defend my beauty; and you,   256
to defend all these; and at all these wards I lie, at a
thousand watches.   258

PANDARUS   Say one of your watches.   259

---

233 *warrant* guarantee 234 *to boot* into the bargain 239 *daws* jackdaws
243 *drayman* cart driver 248 *gentleness* nobility 250 *minced* precious, sim-
pering (here also "cut up into small pieces" as if ready for baking in a pie) 251
no date (lacking dates as vital flavoring); *date is out* (1) stale, past his prime, (2)
impotent 252 *such a woman* (1) so much the woman, (2) so sharp a woman
253 *ward* defensive posture (fencing term) 255 *wiles* escapades (?) 256 *honesty* (1) chastity, (2) good repute; *mask* i.e., facial protection and/or concealment 258 *watches* (1) stages of the night, (2) sleepless nights, (3) times of
vigilance 259 *Say . . . watches* i.e., tell me about just one of those watches

260 CRESSIDA Nay, I'll watch you for that; and that's one of the
261   chiefest of them too. If I cannot ward what I would not
262   have hit, I can watch you for telling how I took the blow,
263   unless it swell past hiding, and then it's past watching.
264 PANDARUS You are such another!
          Enter [Troilus'] Boy.
      BOY Sir, my lord would instantly speak with you.
      PANDARUS Where?
      BOY At your own house. There he unarms him.
      PANDARUS Good boy, tell him I come. *[Exit Boy.]* I
269   doubt he be hurt. Fare ye well, good niece.
270 CRESSIDA Adieu, uncle.
      PANDARUS I will be with you, niece, by and by.
272 CRESSIDA To bring, uncle?
      PANDARUS Ay, a token from Troilus.
274 CRESSIDA By the same token, you are a bawd.
                                        [Exit Pandarus.]
275   Words, vows, gifts, tears, and love's full sacrifice
        He offers in another's enterprise;
        But more in Troilus thousandfold I see
278   Than in the glass of Pandar's praise may be.
279   Yet hold I off. Women are angels, wooing;
280   Things won are done, joy's soul lies in the doing.
281   That she beloved knows nought that knows not this:
282   Men price the thing ungained more than it is;
        That she was never yet, that ever knew
284   Love got so sweet as when desire did sue.
285   Therefore this maxim out of love I teach:
286   Achievement is command; ungained, beseech.

---

260 *watch you* be on my guard against you   **260–61** *one of the chiefest* i.e.,
you are one of the main dangers against which I need to be on guard   **261–
62** *would not have hit* i.e., my virginity   **262** *watch you for telling* make sure
you don't tell   **263** *swell* i.e., from the *blow,* by becoming visibly pregnant;
past watching beyond caution or concealment   **264** *such another* quite a
woman   **269** *doubt* fear   **272** *bring* get even   **274** *bawd* pimp, pander   **275**
sacrifice self-sacrificing devotion   **278** *glass* mirror   **279** *wooing* being wooed
281 *she* i.e., woman   **282** *it is* its real value   **284** *sue* plead   **285** *out of love*
i.e., out of love's book   **286** *Achievement . . . beseech* men command women
once they have gained their love but beg as long as it remains ungained

Then, though my heart's content firm love doth bear,
Nothing of that shall from mine eyes appear.
                              Exit [with Alexander].

                    *

∾ **I.3** *[Sennet.] Enter Agamemnon, Nestor, Ulysses,*
Diomedes, Menelaus, with others.

AGAMEMNON
Princes,
What grief hath set the jaundice on your cheeks?   2
The ample proposition that hope makes   3
In all designs begun on earth below
Fails in the promised largeness. Checks and disasters   5
Grow in the veins of actions highest reared,
As knots, by the conflux of meeting sap,   7
Infects the sound pine and diverts his grain
Tortive and errant from his course of growth.   9
Nor, princes, is it matter new to us   10
That we come short of our suppose so far   11
That after seven years' siege yet Troy walls stand,
Sith every action that hath gone before,   13
Whereof we have record, trial did draw   14
Bias and thwart, not answering the aim
And that unbodied figure of the thought   16
That gave't surmisèd shape. Why then, you princes,
Do you with cheeks abashed behold our works
And call them shames, which are indeed nought else
But the protractive trials of great Jove   20
To find persistive constancy in men,   21

I.3 The Greek camp **s.d.** *Sennet* trumpet call indicating a grand entrance or
procession 2 *grief* trouble, distress; *jaundice* yellow, bilious color 3 *propo-*
sition proposal 5 *Checks* obstacles, setbacks 7 *conflux* confluence (of sap
from many veins of a large tree) 9 *Tortive* distorted; *errant* astray (from its
direct line of growth) 11 *suppose* expectation 13 *Sith* since 14–15
trial . . . thwart i.e., planned actions have always been derailed under the try-
ing conditions of war 16 *unbodied . . . thought* abstract preconception,
mental image 20 *protractive* drawn out 21 *persistive* enduring

The fineness of which metal is not found
In Fortune's love? For then, the bold and coward,
24 The wise and fool, the artist and unread,
25 The hard and soft, seem all affined and kin.
But, in the wind and tempest of her frown,
27 Distinction, with a broad and powerful fan,
Puffing at all, winnows the light away,
And what hath mass or matter by itself
30 Lies rich in virtue and unmingled.

NESTOR
31 With due observance of thy godlike seat,
Great Agamemnon, Nestor shall apply
33 Thy latest words. In the reproof of chance
Lies the true proof of men. The sea being smooth,
35 How many shallow bauble boats dare sail
Upon her patient breast, making their way
With those of nobler bulk!
38 But let the ruffian Boreas once enrage
39 The gentle Thetis, and anon behold
40 The strong-ribbed bark through liquid mountains cut,
41 Bounding between the two moist elements
42 Like Perseus' horse. Where's then the saucy boat,
43 Whose weak untimbered sides but even now
Co-rivaled greatness? Either to harbor fled,
45 Or made a toast for Neptune. Even so
Doth valor's show and valor's worth divide
In storms of fortune. For in her ray and brightness
48 The herd hath more annoyance by the breese
Than by the tiger; but when the splitting wind

---

24 *artist* scholar in the liberal arts   25 *affined* related   27 *fan* shallow basket
for winnowing grain   30 *virtue* essential goodness   31 *seat* throne (i.e.,
supreme eminence)   33 *reproof of chance* i.e., (1) rebuking fickle fortune
through heroic steadfastness, (2) fortune's chastening of humans, who believe they are in control   35 *bauble* like playthings   38 *Boreas* the north
wind in Greek mythology   39 *Thetis* a Nereid or sea-maiden, mother of
Achilles, here personifying the sea   41 *moist elements* i.e., water and air   42
Perseus' horse i.e., his winged horse, Pegasus   43 *untimbered* unsupported by
strong internal beams   45 *toast* a piece of toast floating in liquor (i.e., a
snack for Neptune)   48 *breese* gadfly

Makes flexible the knees of knotted oaks,   50
And flies fled under shade, why then the thing of   51
  courage,
As roused with rage, with rage doth sympathize,   52
And with an accent tuned in selfsame key
Returns to chiding Fortune.   54
ULYSSES   Agamemnon,
Thou great commander, nerves and bone of Greece,   55
Heart of our numbers, soul and only spirit,   56
In whom the tempers and the minds of all
Should be shut up, hear what Ulysses speaks.   58
Besides th' applause and approbation
The which, *[To Agamemnon]* most mighty for thy place 60
  and sway,
    [To Nestor]
And thou most reverend for thy stretched-out life,
I give to both your speeches, which were such
As Agamemnon and the hand of Greece
Should hold up high in brass; and such again   64
As venerable Nestor, hatched in silver,   65
Should with a bond of air, strong as the axletree   66
On which heaven rides, knit all the Greekish ears   67
To his experienced tongue; yet let it please both,
Thou great, and wise, to hear Ulysses speak.
[AGAMEMNON
Speak, Prince of Ithaca; and be't of less expect   70
That matter needless, of importless burden,   71
Divide thy lips than we are confident,
When rank Thersites opes his mastic jaws,   73
We shall hear music, wit, and oracle.]

---

51 *thing of courage* courageous being   52 *As* being; *sympathize* conform
54 *Returns* answers back   55 *nerves* sinews   56 *numbers* army   58 *Should be
shut up* should ideally be incorporated   60 *The which* which; *place and sway*
office and authority   64 *hold . . . brass* i.e., hold up as elocutionary models
inscribed in brass   65 *hatched in silver* with silver streaks in his hair   66
bond of air invisible bond created by the eloquence of Nestor's speech; *axletree* axis   67 *rides* turns   70 *of less expect* less to be expected   71 *importless*
no importance   73 *rank* foul; *mastic* champing, laboring (possibly scathing)

ULYSSES

75 Troy, yet upon his basis, had been down,
And the great Hector's sword had lacked a master,
77 But for these instances.
78 The specialty of rule hath been neglected;
And look, how many Grecian tents do stand
80 Hollow upon this plain, so many hollow factions.
81 When that the general is not like the hive
82 To whom the foragers shall all repair,
83 What honey is expected? Degree being vizarded,
Th' unworthiest shows as fairly in the mask.
85 The heavens themselves, the planets, and this center
86 Observe degree, priority, and place,
87 Insisture, course, proportion, season, form,
88 Office, and custom, in all line of order.
89 And therefore is the glorious planet Sol
90 In noble eminence enthroned and sphered
91 Amidst the other; whose med'cinable eye
92 Corrects the influence of evil planets,
93 And posts, like the commandment of a king,
94 Sans check to good and bad. But when the planets
In evil mixture to disorder wander,
96 What plagues and what portents, what mutiny,
What raging of the sea, shaking of earth,
Commotion in the winds, frights, changes, horrors,
99 Divert and crack, rend and deracinate
100 The unity and married calm of states
101 Quite from their fixure? O, when degree is shaked,

---

75 *basis* foundation   77 *instances* causes, considerations   78 *specialty of rule* prerogatives of authority   80 *Hollow* empty, without real content   81 *general* political community, state   82 *repair* return (as contributors)   83–84 *Degree . . . mask* when proper rank and distinction are obscured, the least worthy look as good in their masks as the most worthy   85 *center* i.e., the earth as supposed center of the universe   86 *place* proper station   87 *Insisture* regularity of position   88 *line* rank   89 *Sol* the sun   90 *sphered* i.e., placed in its heavenly sphere (the highest)   91 *med'cinable* healing   92 *influence* astrological effect   93 *posts* speeds   94 *Sans check* unimpeded; *to good and bad* i.e., supporting the good and curbing the bad   96 *portents* ill omens, monstrosities   99 *deracinate* uproot   101 *fixure* stability

Which is the ladder of all high designs,
The enterprise is sick. How could communities,
Degrees in schools, and brotherhoods in cities,   104
Peaceful commerce from dividable shores,   105
The primogenity and due of birth,   106
Prerogative of age, crowns, scepters, laurels,
But by degree, stand in authentic place?   108
Take but degree away, untune that string,
And hark what discord follows. Each thing meets   *110*
In mere oppugnancy. The bounded waters   111
Should lift their bosoms higher than the shores
And make a sop of all this solid globe;   113
Strength should be lord of imbecility,   114
And the rude son should strike his father dead;   115
Force should be right; or rather right and wrong,
Between whose endless jar justice resides,   117
Should lose their names, and so should justice too.
Then everything include itself in power,   119
Power into will, will into appetite;   *120*
And appetite, an universal wolf,
So doubly seconded with will and power,   122
Must make perforce an universal prey   123
And last eat up himself. Great Agamemnon,
This chaos, when degree is suffocate,
Follows the choking.
And this neglection of degree it is   127
That by a pace goes backward with a purpose   128
It hath to climb. The general's disdained
By him one step below, he by the next,   *130*

---

104 *Degrees* academic ranks; *brotherhoods* trade guilds   105 *dividable* separate (i.e., potentially antagonistic)   106 *primogenity* (a different form of the
more regular "primogeniture," the doctrine that the eldest son is the lawful
inheritor)   108 *authentic* legitimate   111 *mere oppugnancy* total strife   113
sop saturated gobbet (e.g., toast in wine)   114 *should* would; *imbecility* weakness   115 *rude* boorish, uncivilized   117 *jar* collision   119 *include . . .
power* (would) terminate or be subsumed in power   122 *seconded* backed up
123 *prey* act of devouring   127 *neglection* neglect   128–29 *by a pace . . .
climb* i.e., everything goes backward, step by step, although the intent is to
ascend

That next by him beneath; so every step,
132   Exampled by the first pace that is sick
        Of his superior, grows to an envious fever
134   Of pale and bloodless emulation:
        And 'tis this fever that keeps Troy on foot,
        Not her own sinews. To end a tale of length,
        Troy in our weakness stands, not in her strength.

NESTOR
138   Most wisely hath Ulysses here discovered
        The fever whereof all our power is sick.

AGAMEMNON
140   The nature of the sickness found, Ulysses,
        What is the remedy?

ULYSSES
        The great Achilles, whom opinion crowns
143   The sinew and the forehand of our host,
        Having his ear full of his airy fame,
145   Grows dainty of his worth, and in his tent
        Lies mocking our designs. With him Patroclus
        Upon a lazy bed the livelong day
148   Breaks scurril jests,
        And with ridiculous and silly action
150   (Which, slanderer, he imitation calls)
151   He pageants us. Sometime, great Agamemnon,
152   Thy topless deputation he puts on
153   And, like a strutting player, whose conceit
154   Lies in his hamstring, and doth think it rich
155   To hear the wooden dialogue and sound
156   'Twixt his stretched footing and the scaffoldage,

132–33 *Exampled . . . superior* finding an example in the first step someone
enviously takes against a superior   134 *emulation* envious resentment of su-
periors   138 *discovered* revealed, diagnosed   143 *forehand* mainstay   145
dainty finicky, sparing   148 *scurril* scurrilous   151 *pageants* acts (parodically
mimics)   152 *topless deputation* supreme authority   153 *conceit* wit, ideas
154 *hamstring* tendon at the back of the knee   155 *wooden* lifeless (also possibly implies resonating in a wooden theater)   156 *stretched footing* exaggerated strides; *scaffoldage* stage

Such to-be-pitied and o'erwrested seeming   157
He acts thy greatness in; and when he speaks,
'Tis like a chime a-mending, with terms unsquared,   159
Which from the tongue of roaring Typhon dropped   160
Would seem hyperboles. At this fusty stuff   161
The large Achilles, on his pressed bed lolling,
From his deep chest laughs out a loud applause,
Cries, "Excellent! 'tis Agamemnon right.
Now play me Nestor; hem, and stroke thy beard,   165
As he being drest to some oration."   166
That's done, as near as the extremest ends   167
Of parallels, as like as Vulcan and his wife,   168
Yet god Achilles still cries, "Excellent!
'Tis Nestor right. Now play him me, Patroclus,   170
Arming to answer in a night alarm."   171
And then, forsooth, the faint defects of age   172
Must be the scene of mirth; to cough and spit,   173
And with a palsy fumbling on his gorget,   174
Shake in and out the rivet. And at this sport   175
Sir Valor dies; cries, "O! enough, Patroclus,
Or give me ribs of steel! I shall split all
In pleasure of my spleen." And in this fashion   178
All our abilities, gifts, natures, shapes,
Severals and generals of grace exact,   180
Achievements, plots, orders, preventions,   181
Excitements to the field or speech for truce,   182
Success or loss, what is or is not, serves

---

157 *o'erwrested seeming* overdone simulation   159 *chime* set of bells; *unsquared* unsuited   160 *Typhon* mythical monster with serpents' heads and a tremendous voice   161 *fusty* stale, overblown   165 *hem* clear the throat   166 *drest* prepared for   167–68 *the extremest . . . parallels* i.e., far apart, since parallels never intersect   168 *Vulcan and his wife* the lame, sooty fire god Vulcan and his beautiful wife, Venus, in Roman mythology   170 *play him me* play him for me   171 *answer* respond   172 *faint* weakening   173 *scene of mirth* comic scene   174 *palsy* palsied; *gorget* throat armor   175 *rivet* fastening   178 *spleen* (organ of laughter in traditional physiology)   180 *Severals . . . exact* individual and common excellences   181 *plots* strategic plans; *preventions* precautions   182 *Excitements* incentives, exhortations

184   As stuff for these two to make paradoxes.

NESTOR
       And in the imitation of these twain,
       Who, as Ulysses says, opinion crowns
187   With an imperial voice, many are infect.
       Ajax is grown self-willed, and bears his head
189   In such a rein, in full as proud a place,
190   As broad Achilles; keeps his tent like him;
191   Makes factious feasts; rails on our state of war
       Bold as an oracle, and sets Thersites,
193   A slave whose gall coins slanders like a mint,
       To match us in comparisons with dirt,
195   To weaken and discredit our exposure,
196   How rank soever rounded in with danger.

ULYSSES
197   They tax our policy and call it cowardice,
198   Count wisdom as no member of the war,
199   Forestall prescience, and esteem no act
200   But that of hand. The still and mental parts
       That do contrive how many hands shall strike
202   When fitness calls them on, and know by measure
       Of their observant toil the enemies' weight –
       Why, this hath not a finger's dignity.
205   They call this bed work, mapp'ry, closet war;
       So that the ram that batters down the wall,
207   For the great swinge and rudeness of his poise,
       They place before his hand that made the engine,
209   Or those that with the fineness of their souls

---

184 *paradoxes* absurdities   187 *infect* infected   189 *In such a rein* so uplifted
190 *broad* (1) large-framed, (2) coarse   191 *factious* (1) fomenting dissen-
sion, (2) factional; *rails . . . war* declaims against our military posture   193
gall bitterness, insolence   195 *exposure* exposed situation   196 *How
rank . . . danger* i.e., no matter how grave the dangers surrounding us   197
tax criticize   198 *member* constituent part   199 *Forestall prescience* discount
foresight   202 *measure* means, calculation   205 *bed work* i.e., unsoldierly
action; *mapp'ry* mapmaking; *closet war* war made in the study (i.e., not on
the battlefield)   207 *swinge and rudeness* impetus and brute force   209 *souls*
intellect

By reason guide his execution.   210

NESTOR
Let this be granted, and Achilles' horse   211
Makes many Thetis' sons.   212
    [*Tucket.*]

AGAMEMNON
What trumpet? Look, Menelaus.

MENELAUS
From Troy.
    [*Enter Aeneas.*]

AGAMEMNON
What would you 'fore our tent?

AENEAS
Is this great Agamemnon's tent, I pray you?

AGAMEMNON
Even this.

AENEAS
May one that is a herald and a prince
Do a fair message to his kingly eyes?   219

AGAMEMNON
With surety stronger than Achilles' arm   220
'Fore all the Greekish heads, which with one voice   221
Call Agamemnon head and general.

AENEAS
Fair leave and large security. How may   223
A stranger to those most imperial looks
Know them from eyes of other mortals?

AGAMEMNON   How?

AENEAS
Ay.
I ask, that I might waken reverence,   227
And bid the cheek be ready with a blush

211–12 *Let . . . sons* i.e., (1) if that is granted, Achilles' horse counts for a
great deal more than Achilles, son of Thetis, (2) Achilles' mass of horsemen,
the Myrmidons, do so   212 **s.d.** *Tucket* trumpet call   219 *fair* courteous,
civil   221 *'Fore* going before, as a leader   223 *leave* permission; *security* guarantee   227 *waken reverence* awaken due respect

Modest as morning when she coldly eyes
230   The youthful Phoebus,
231   Which is that god in office, guiding men?
       Which is the high and mighty Agamemnon?

AGAMEMNON
       This Trojan scorns us, or the men of Troy
       Are ceremonious courtiers.

AENEAS
235   Courtiers as free, as debonair, unarmed,
236   As bending angels; that's their fame in peace.
237   But when they would seem soldiers, they have galls,
238   Good arms, strong joints, true swords; and, Jove's ac-
           cord,
239   Nothing so full of heart. But peace, Aeneas;
240   Peace, Trojan; lay thy finger on thy lips.
241   The worthiness of praise distains his worth,
       If that the praised himself bring the praise forth.
243   But what the repining enemy commends,
244   That breath fame blows; that praise, sole pure, tran-
           scends.

AGAMEMNON
       Sir, you of Troy, call you yourself Aeneas?

AENEAS
       Ay, Greek, that is my name.

AGAMEMNON
       What's your affair, I pray you?

AENEAS
       Sir, pardon; 'tis for Agamemnon's ears.

AGAMEMNON
       He hears nought privately that comes from Troy.

---

230 *Phoebus* Apollo, the sun god   231 *god in office* i.e., god by virtue of his
regal function   235 *free* generous; *debonair* gracious   236 *bending* courteously bowing down; *fame* reputation   237 *galls* proudly aggressive spirits
238 *Jove's accord* Jove being in accord   239 *Nothing . . . heart* unequaled in
courage   241–42 *The worthiness . . . forth* (1) deserved praise taints the one
to whom it applies, (2) it becomes tainted when he praises himself   243 *repining* grudging   244 *breath fame blows* i.e., personified fame trumpets this
praise abroad; *sole* solely

AENEAS
　　Nor I from Troy come not to whisper with him:　　　250
　　I bring a trumpet to awake his ear,
　　To set his seat on the attentive bent,　　　252
　　And then to speak.　　　253
AGAMEMNON　　　　Speak frankly as the wind;
　　It is not Agamemnon's sleeping hour.
　　That thou shalt know, Trojan, he is awake,
　　He tells thee so himself.　　　256
AENEAS　　　　　　　　　Trumpet, blow loud,
　　Send thy brass voice through all these lazy tents;
　　And every Greek of mettle, let him know,
　　What Troy means fairly shall be spoke aloud.　　　259
　　　Sound trumpet.
　　We have, great Agamemnon, here in Troy　　　260
　　A prince called Hector – Priam is his father –
　　Who in this dull and long-continued truce
　　Is resty grown. He bade me take a trumpet,　　　263
　　And to this purpose speak: Kings, princes, lords,
　　If there be one among the fair'st of Greece
　　That holds his honor higher than his ease,
　　That seeks his praise more than he fears his peril,
　　That knows his valor and knows not his fear,
　　That loves his mistress more than in confession　　　269
　　With truant vows to her own lips he loves,　　　270
　　And dare avow her beauty and her worth
　　In other arms than hers – to him this challenge.
　　Hector, in view of Trojans and of Greeks,
　　Shall make it good, or do his best to do it,　　　274
　　He hath a lady wiser, fairer, truer,
　　Than ever Greek did compass in his arms;　　　276
　　And will tomorrow with his trumpet call,
　　Midway between your tents and walls of Troy,

---

252 *set . . . bent* i.e., to gain his official attention　253 *frankly* freely　256 *Trumpet* trumpeter　259 *fairly* civilly　263 *resty* restive　269 *in confession* in mere profession　270 *truant* faithless　274 *make it good* back it up　276 *compass* embrace

To rouse a Grecian that is true in love.
280   If any come, Hector shall honor him;
If none, he'll say in Troy when he retires,
282   The Grecian dames are sunburnt and not worth
283   The splinter of a lance. Even so much.

AGAMEMNON
This shall be told our lovers, Lord Aeneas;
285   If none of them have soul in such a kind,
We left them all at home. But we are soldiers;
287   And may that soldier a mere recreant prove,
That means not, hath not, or is not in love.
If then one is, or hath, or means to be,
290   That one meets Hector; if none else, I am he.

NESTOR
Tell him of Nestor, one that was a man
292   When Hector's grandsire sucked. He is old now,
But if there be not in our Grecian host
A noble man that hath one spark of fire
To answer for his love, tell him from me,
296   I'll hide my silver beard in a gold beaver,
297   And in my vambrace put this withered brawn,
And, meeting him, will tell him that my lady
299   Was fairer than his grandam, and as chaste
300   As may be in the world. His youth in flood,
301   I'll prove this troth with my three drops of blood.

AENEAS
302   Now heavens forfend such scarcity of youth!

ULYSSES
Amen.

[AGAMEMNON]
Fair Lord Aeneas, let me touch your hand;
To our pavilion shall I lead you first.
Achilles shall have word of this intent;

---

282 *sunburnt* dark (implying ugly, as opposed to "fair") 283 *splinter* (1) splinter, (2) splintering 285 *in such a kind* of that (noble) nature 287 *recreant* traitor 292 *grandsire* grandfather 296 *beaver* face guard of a helmet 297 *vambrace* plating for the forearm 299 *grandam* grandmother 300 *in flood* at its peak 301 *prove this troth* test his faith 302 *forfend* forbid

So shall each lord of Greece, from tent to tent.
Yourself shall feast with us before you go,
And find the welcome of a noble foe.   309
                     [Exeunt. Manent Ulysses and Nestor.]

ULYSSES
  Nestor.   310
NESTOR
  What says Ulysses?
ULYSSES
  I have a young conception in my brain;   312
  Be you my time to bring it to some shape.
NESTOR
  What is't?
ULYSSES
  [This 'tis:]
  Blunt wedges rive hard knots; the seeded pride   316
  That hath to this maturity blown up   317
  In rank Achilles, must or now be cropped   318
  Or, shedding, breed a nursery of like evil   319
  To overbulk us all.   320
NESTOR   Well, and how?
ULYSSES
  This challenge that the gallant Hector sends,
  However it is spread in general name,   322
  Relates in purpose only to Achilles.
NESTOR
  True, the purpose is perspicuous as substance   324
  Whose grossness little characters sum up;
  And, in the publication, make no strain   326
  But that Achilles, were his brain as barren

---

309 s.d. *Manent* remain   **312–13** *I . . . shape* i.e., I have a new idea – give me
your time (or play the role of time) while I develop it   **316** *Blunt* powerful (?);
rive split; *seeded* implanted   **317** *blown up* (1) grown up, (2) expanded   **318**
rank loathsomely overgrown; *cropped* cut back   **318–19** *or . . . Or* either . . . or
319 *shedding* scattering seed   **320** *overbulk* (1) outgrow, (2) overshadow   **322**
spread . . . name addressed to the public   **324–25** *perspicuous . . . up* as evident as large entities whose magnitude is expressed by small figures   **326**
in . . . strain don't doubt that in the announcement

328   As banks of Libya – though, Apollo knows,
        'Tis dry enough – will with great speed of judgment,
330   Ay with celerity, find Hector's purpose
        Pointing on him.

ULYSSES
        And wake him to the answer, think you?

NESTOR
333   Why, 'tis most meet. Who may you else oppose
334   That can from Hector bring his honor off,
        If not Achilles? Though't be a sportful combat,
336   Yet in the trial much opinion dwells;
        For here the Trojans taste our dear'st repute
        With their fin'st palate; and trust to me, Ulysses,
339   Our imputation shall be oddly poised
340   In this vild action. For the success,
341   Although particular, shall give a scantling
342   Of good or bad unto the general,
343   And in such indexes, although small pricks
        To their subsequent volumes, there is seen
345   The baby figure of the giant mass
        Of things to come at large. It is supposed
        He that meets Hector issues from our choice;
        And choice, being mutual act of all our souls,
349   Makes merit her election, and doth boil,
350   As 'twere from forth us all, a man distilled
351   Out of our virtues; who miscarrying,
352   What heart receives from hence a conquering part,
353   To steel a strong opinion to themselves!
354   [Which entertained, limbs are his instruments,

---

328 *banks* shores (dunes?)   **333** *meet* fitting   **334** *bring . . . off* come out
with honor intact   **336** *opinion* reputation   **339** *imputation . . . poised* reputation will be exposed to exceptionally high risk   **340** *vild* trivial; *success* outcome   **341** *scantling* sample   **342** *general* entire army   **343–44** *small . . .
volumes* small marks in comparison with the volumes to follow   **345** *baby
figure* (1) infant image, (2) diminutive projection   **349** *election* the basis of
choice   **351** *miscarrying* failing   **352** *conquering part* victorious image or
role   **353** *to* of   **354** *his* i.e., the strong opinion's

In no less working than are swords and bows   355
Directive by the limbs.]   356

ULYSSES
Give pardon to my speech: therefore 'tis meet
Achilles meet not Hector. Let us, like merchants,
First show foul wares, and think perchance they'll sell;   359
If not, the luster of the better shall exceed   360
By showing the worse first. Do not consent
That ever Hector and Achilles meet;
For both our honor and our shame in this
Are dogged with two strange followers.   364

NESTOR
I see them not with my old eyes. What are they?

ULYSSES
What glory our Achilles shares from Hector,   366
Were he not proud, we all should share with him.
But he already is too insolent,
And we were better parch in Afric sun   369
Than in the pride and salt scorn of his eyes,   370
Should he scape Hector fair. If he were foiled,   371
Why then we did our main opinion crush   372
In taint of our best man. No, make a lott'ry,   373
And by device let blockish Ajax draw   374
The sort to fight with Hector; among ourselves   375
Give him allowance for the better man,   376
For that will physic the great Myrmidon   377
Who broils in loud applause, and make him fall   378
His crest that prouder than blue Iris bends.   379
If the dull brainless Ajax come safe off,   380

---

355 *In no less working* (1) works no less, (2) works no less effectively 356
Directive directed 359 *foul* inferior 364 *strange followers* i.e., undesirable
consequences (either Achilles' victory or defeat would be unwelcome) 366
shares from gains from 369 *Afric* African 370 *salt* bitter 371 *scape . . .
fair* come off well 372 *main opinion* chief source of our reputation 373
taint dishonoring 374 *device* trick 375 *sort* lot 376 *allowance* credit
377 *physic* purge (of his pride); *Myrmidon* (Achilles' followers, mythically descended from a swarm of ants [Greek *myrmes*] were known as Myrmidons)
378 *broils* basks; *fall* lower 379 *Iris* rainbow

381 We'll dress him up in voices; if he fail,
   Yet go we under our opinion still
   That we have better men. But, hit or miss,
384 Our project's life this shape of sense assumes:
   Ajax employed plucks down Achilles' plumes.
NESTOR
   Now, Ulysses, I begin to relish thy advice,
   And I will give a taste thereof forthwith
   To Agamemnon. Go we to him straight.
   Two curs shall tame each other; pride alone
390 Must tarre the mastiffs on, as 'twere a bone. *Exeunt.*

           *

ᴥ **II.1** *Enter Ajax and Thersites.*

AJAX Thersites!
2 THERSITES Agamemnon – how if he had biles, full, all
  over, generally?
  AJAX Thersites!
5 THERSITES And those biles did run – say so – did not
6 the general run, then? Were not that a botchy core?
  AJAX Dog!
  THERSITES Then would come some matter from him. I
  see none now.
10 AJAX Thou bitch wolf's son, canst thou not hear? Feel
  then.
   [Strikes him.]
12 THERSITES The plague of Greece upon thee, thou mongrel beef-witted lord!

---

381 *voices* flattering opinions **384** *shape of sense* definite outline **390** *tarre*
incite
 II.1 The Greek camp **2** *biles* boils **5** *say so* let us imagine that **6** *gen-eral run* (Agamemnon as *general* will be "running"; the army as a whole will
run away); *botchy core* infected center of a boil (possibly an army without the
heart to fight) **12** *plague of Greece* (possible allusion to the plague, mentioned in Homer's *Iliad*, visited on the Greek army by Apollo)

AJAX   Speak then, thou vinewed'st leaven, speak. I will   14
beat thee into handsomeness.

THERSITES   I shall sooner rail thee into wit and holiness;
but I think thy horse will sooner con an oration than   17
thou learn a prayer without book. Thou canst strike,   18
canst thou? A red murrain o' thy jade's tricks!   19

AJAX   Toadstool, learn me the proclamation.   20

THERSITES   Dost thou think I have no sense, thou strik-   21
est me thus?

AJAX   The proclamation!

THERSITES   Thou art proclaimed fool, I think.

AJAX   Do not, porpentine, do not; my fingers itch.   25

THERSITES   I would thou didst itch from head to foot.
An I had the scratching of thee, I would make thee the   27
loathsomest scab in Greece. When thou art forth in the
incursions, thou strikest as slow as another.   29

AJAX   I say, the proclamation!   *30*

THERSITES   Thou grumblest and railest every hour on
Achilles, and thou art as full of envy at his greatness as
Cerberus is at Proserpina's beauty, ay, that thou bark'st   33
at him.

AJAX   Mistress Thersites!   35

THERSITES   Thou shouldst strike him.

AJAX   Cobloaf!   37

THERSITES   He would pun thee into shivers with his fist,   38
as a sailor breaks a biscuit.

AJAX   You whoreson cur!   40
     [Beating him]

THERSITES   Do, do.   41

---

14 *vinewed'st leaven* moldiest dough added to fresh dough to begin fermentation   17 *con* memorize   18 *without book* by heart   19 *murrain* plague;
jade broken-down but cunningly uncooperative horse   20 *learn me* find out
for me   21 *sense* power of sensation   25 *porpentine* porcupine   27 *An* if
29 *incursions* military sallies   33 *Cerberus* three-headed dog guarding the entrance to Hades in Greek mythology; *Proserpina* beautiful bride of Pluto in
the underworld   35 *Mistress* (insult to Thersites' masculinity)   37 *Cobloaf*
small, lumpy breadloaf   38 *pun* pound; *shivers* splinters   40 *whoreson* bastard (common term of abuse)   41 *Do, do* keep it up

42 AJAX Thou stool for a witch!

THERSITES Ay, do, do! Thou sodden-witted lord, thou
hast no more brain than I have in mine elbows; an
45 asinico may tutor thee. Thou scurvy-valiant ass, thou
46 art here but to thrash Trojans, and thou art bought and
sold among those of any wit like a barbarian slave. If
48 thou use to beat me, I will begin at thy heel, and tell
49 what thou art by inches, thou thing of no bowels, thou!

50 AJAX You dog!

THERSITES You scurvy lord!

AJAX You cur!
[Beating him]

53 THERSITES Mars his idiot! Do, rudeness; do, camel;
do, do!
[Enter Achilles and Patroclus.]

ACHILLES Why, how now, Ajax, wherefore do ye thus?
How now, Thersites, what's the matter, man?

THERSITES You see him there, do you?

ACHILLES Ay, what's the matter?

THERSITES Nay, look upon him.

60 ACHILLES So I do. What's the matter?

THERSITES Nay, but regard him well.

ACHILLES Well, why, so I do.

THERSITES But yet you look not well upon him; for,
64 whosomever you take him to be, he is Ajax.

ACHILLES I know that, fool.

THERSITES Ay, but that fool knows not himself.

AJAX Therefore I beat thee.

68 THERSITES Lo, lo, lo, lo, what modicums of wit he ut-
69 ters! His evasions have ears thus long. I have bobbed his
70 brain more than he has beat my bones. I will buy nine
71 sparrows for a penny, and his pia mater is not worth the

---

42 *stool* privy 45 *asinico* little ass; *scurvy-valiant* despicably heroic 46
thrash beat, mow down 46–47 *bought and sold* traded, used 48 *use to*
make it a habit 49 *bowels* i.e., capacity for feeling, compassion 53 *Mars
his* Mars's 64 *whosomever* whomsoever 68 *modicums* small quantities 69
evasions attempts at repartee; *ears . . . long* i.e., ass's ears; *bobbed* thumped
71 *pia mater* i.e., brain (from the membrane surrounding the brain)

ninth part of a sparrow. This lord, Achilles – Ajax, who
wears his wit in his belly and his guts in his head – I'll
tell you what I say of him.

ACHILLES　What?

THERSITES　I say, this Ajax –
　　[Ajax threatens to strike him.]

ACHILLES　Nay, good Ajax.

THERSITES　Has not so much wit –
　　[Ajax again threatens to strike him.]

ACHILLES　Nay, I must hold you.

THERSITES　As will stop the eye of Helen's needle, for　80
whom he comes to fight.

ACHILLES　Peace, fool!

THERSITES　I would have peace and quietness, but the
fool will not – he there, that he. Look you there.

AJAX　O thou damned cur, I shall –

ACHILLES　Will you set your wit to a fool's?　　　　86

THERSITES　No, I warrant you, the fool's will shame it.

PATROCLUS　Good words, Thersites.　　　　　　88

ACHILLES　What's the quarrel?

AJAX　I bade the vile owl go learn me the tenor of the　90
proclamation, and he rails upon me.

THERSITES　I serve thee not.

AJAX　Well, go to, go to.

THERSITES　I serve here voluntary.

ACHILLES　Your last service was sufferance, 'twas not vol-　95
untary; no man is beaten voluntary. Ajax was here the
voluntary, and you as under an impress.　　　　97

THERSITES　E'en so! A great deal of your wit, too, lies in
your sinews, or else there be liars. Hector shall have a
great catch if he knock out either of your brains. A were　100
as good crack a fusty nut with no kernel.

ACHILLES　What, with me too, Thersites?

---

80 *stop* fill　86 *set your wit* match your wits　88 *Good words* speak civilly
95 *sufferance* (1) suffering, (2) enforced servitude　97 *impress* conscription
100–1 *A were as good* he might as well

THERSITES There's Ulysses and old Nestor – whose wit was moldy ere your grandsires had nails on their toes – yoke you like draft oxen and make you plow up the wars.

ACHILLES What? What?

108 THERSITES Yes, good sooth. To, Achilles! To, Ajax, to –

AJAX I shall cut out your tongue.

110 THERSITES 'Tis no matter. I shall speak as much as thou afterwards.

PATROCLUS No more words, Thersites. Peace!

113 THERSITES I will hold my peace when Achilles' brach bids me, shall I?

ACHILLES There's for you, Patroclus.

116 THERSITES I will see you hanged, like clotpoles, ere I come any more to your tents. I will keep where there is

118 wit stirring and leave the faction of fools.   *Exit.*

PATROCLUS A good riddance.

ACHILLES

120 Marry, this, sir, is proclaimed through all our host:

121 That Hector, by the fifth hour of the sun,
Will, with a trumpet, 'twixt our tents and Troy
Tomorrow morning call some knight to arms

124 That hath a stomach, and such a one that dare
Maintain – I know not what; 'tis trash. Farewell.

AJAX

Farewell? Who shall answer him?

ACHILLES

I know not. 'Tis put to lott'ry. Otherwise,

128 He knew his man.

AJAX

O, meaning you? I will go learn more of it.   *[Exeunt.]*

✳

---

108 *good sooth* truly; *To . . . to* (imitates the driver of an ox team)   113 *brach* bitch (implying that Patroclus is Achilles' male whore)   116 *clotpoles* blockheads   118 *faction* company   120 *Marry* (contraction of "by the Virgin Mary")   121 *fifth hour* 11 AM   124 *stomach* courage   128 *knew* would know

∾ **II.2** *Enter Priam, Hector, Troilus, Paris, and Helenus.*

PRIAM
    After so many hours, lives, speeches spent,
    Thus once again says Nestor from the Greeks:
    "Deliver Helen, and all damage else,
    As honor, loss of time, travail, expense,
    Wounds, friends, and what else dear that is consumed
    In hot digestion of this cormorant war,   6
    Shall be struck off." Hector, what say you to't?   7
HECTOR
    Though no man lesser fears the Greeks than I,
    As far as toucheth my particular,   9
    Yet, dread Priam,   10
    There is no lady of more softer bowels,   11
    More spongy to suck in the sense of fear,
    More ready to cry out "Who knows what follows?"
    Than Hector is. The wound of peace is surety,   14
    Surety secure; but modest doubt is called
    The beacon of the wise, the tent that searches   16
    To th' bottom of the worst. Let Helen go.
    Since the first sword was drawn about this question,   18
    Every tithe soul, 'mongst many thousand dismes,   19
    Hath been as dear as Helen; I mean, of ours.   20
    If we have lost so many tenths of ours
    To guard a thing not ours nor worth to us   22
    (Had it our name) the value of one ten,   23
    What merit's in that reason which denies   24
    The yielding of her up?

———

II.2 Priam's palace **6** *cormorant* ravenous (derived from the cormorant as a proverbially greedy bird) **7** *struck off* canceled **9** *toucheth . . . particular* affects me personally **11** *softer bowels* compassionate nature **14** *wound* injury **14–15** *surety . . . secure* complacent confidence **16** *tent* cloth swab for cleaning out wounds **18** *question* cause of dispute **19** *Every . . . dismes* every tenth soul (taken by war) among many thousand such tenths **20** *dear* valuable **22** *worth* possessing value **23** *Had . . . name* if it were ours (if she were Trojan); *one ten* i.e., one Trojan life **24** *reason* argument

TROILUS   Fie, fie, my brother!
    Weigh you the worth and honor of a king
    So great as our dread father in a scale
28   Of common ounces? Will you with counters sum
29   The past-proportion of his infinite,
30   And buckle in a waist most fathomless
31   With spans and inches so diminutive
    As fears and reasons? Fie, for godly shame!

HELENUS
33   No marvel, though you bite so sharp at reasons,
    You are so empty of them. Should not our father
35   Bear the great sway of his affairs with reason,
    Because your speech hath none that tell him so?

TROILUS
    You are for dreams and slumbers, brother priest;
38   You fur your gloves with reason. Here are your reasons:
    You know an enemy intends you harm;
40   You know a sword employed is perilous,
41   And reason flies the object of all harm.
    Who marvels then, when Helenus beholds
    A Grecian and his sword, if he do set
    The very wings of reason to his heels
45   And fly like chidden Mercury from Jove,
46   Or like a star disorbed? Nay, if we talk of reason,
    Let's shut our gates and sleep. Manhood and honor
48   Should have hare hearts, would they but fat their
      thoughts
    With this crammed reason. Reason and respect
50   Make livers pale and lustihood deject.

---

28 *with counters sum* compute with worthless tokens   29 *past . . . infinite* his immeasurable greatness   30 *fathomless* incalculable   31 *spans* measures of nine inches   33 *No marvel* no wonder   35 *sway* command   38 *fur your gloves* i.e., use reason to make things easy and comfortable   41 *object of all harm* any harmful object   45 *chidden* rebuked, scolded; *Mercury* the messenger of the gods in Roman mythology, equivalent to the Greek Hermes, imagined to have winged feet; *Jove* king of the gods in Roman mythology, equivalent to the Greek Zeus   46 *disorbed* thrown from its sphere   48 *Should* would; *would they* if they were to   50 *livers* (the liver was regarded as the seat of the passions); *lustihood deject* i.e., depress physical vitality

HECTOR
  Brother, she is not worth what she doth cost
  The keeping.
TROILUS   What's aught but as 'tis valued?
HECTOR
  But value dwells not in particular will;   53
  It holds his estimate and dignity   54
  As well wherein 'tis precious of itself
  As in the prizer. 'Tis mad idolatry   56
  To make the service greater than the god;
  And the will dotes that is attributive   58
  To what infectiously itself affects,
  Without some image of th' affected merit.   60
TROILUS
  I take today a wife, and my election   61
  Is led on in the conduct of my will,   62
  My will enkindled by mine eyes and ears,
  Two traded pilots 'twixt the dangerous shores   64
  Of will and judgment. How may I avoid,   65
  Although my will distaste what it elected,
  The wife I chose? There can be no evasion
  To blench from this and to stand firm by honor.   68
  We turn not back the silks upon the merchant
  When we have soiled them, nor the remainder viands   70
  We do not throw in unrespective sieve   71
  Because we now are full. It was thought meet   72
  Paris should do some vengeance on the Greeks.
  Your breath with full consent bellied his sails;   74
  The seas and winds, old wranglers, took a truce   75
  And did him service; he touched the ports desired,   76

---

53 *particular will* individual inclination   54 *dignity* worth   56 *prizer* appraiser   58–59 *will . . . affects* the will is infatuated that subjects itself to what it pathologically desires   60 *Without . . . merit* without some discernible evidence of value in what is desired   61 *election* choice   62 *conduct* direction   64 *traded* experienced   65 *avoid* get rid of   68 *blench* shrink   70 *viands* foodstuffs   71 *unrespective sieve* common receptacle for leftovers   72 *meet* proper   74 *bellied* swelled   75 *old wranglers* longstanding antagonists   76 *touched* docked at

77	And for an old aunt whom the Greeks held captive
78	He brought a Grecian queen, whose youth and fresh-
	ness
79	Wrinkles Apollo's and makes stale the morning.
80	Why keep we her? The Grecians keep our aunt.
	Is she worth keeping? Why, she is a pearl
82	Whose price hath launched above a thousand ships
	And turned crowned kings to merchants.
84	If you'll avouch 'twas wisdom Paris went –
	As you must needs, for you all cried, "Go, go" –
	If you'll confess he brought home worthy prize –
	As you must needs, for you all clapped your hands,
	And cried, "Inestimable!" – why do you now
89	The issue of your proper wisdoms rate,
90	And do a deed that never Fortune did,
91	Beggar the estimation which you prized
	Richer than sea and land? O theft most base,
	That we have stol'n what we do fear to keep!
94	But thieves unworthy of a thing so stol'n,
	That in their country did them that disgrace
	We fear to warrant in our native place.

CASSANDRA   *[Within]*
| 97 | Cry, Trojans, cry! |

PRIAM   What noise? What shriek is this?

TROILUS
'Tis our mad sister. I do know her voice.

CASSANDRA   *[Within]* Cry, Trojans!

| 100 | HECTOR   It is Cassandra. |

Enter Cassandra [with her hair about her ears].

---

77 *aunt* i.e., Hesione, Priam's sister, the mother of Ajax, who had been forcibly married to the Greek Telamon   78 *Grecian queen* i.e., Helen of Troy   79 *Apollo* the sun god, eternally youthful   82 *Whose . . . ships* (echoes a famous description of Helen in Christopher Marlowe's *Dr. Faustus*)   84 *avouch* maintain   89 *issue . . . wisdoms rate* condemn the outcomes (progeny) of your own wisdom   91 *Beggar the estimation* drastically devalue   94–96 *But thieves . . . native place* but (we are) thieves so unworthy that, having done them shame in their own country, we fear to justify our deed at home   97 *Cry . . . cry* (Cassandra's fate, decreed by Apollo, is to have her prophecies ignored)

CASSANDRA
    Cry, Trojans, cry! Lend me ten thousand eyes,
    And I will fill them with prophetic tears.
HECTOR
    Peace, sister, peace!
CASSANDRA
    Virgins and boys, mid-age and wrinkled elders,
    Soft infancy, that nothing canst but cry,
    Add to my clamors! Let us pay betimes   106
    A moiety of that mass of moan to come.   107
    Cry, Trojans, cry! Practice your eyes with tears!   108
    Troy must not be, nor goodly Ilion stand;
    Our firebrand brother, Paris, burns us all.   *110*
    Cry, Trojans, cry! A Helen and a woe!
    Cry, cry! Troy burns, or else let Helen go.   *Exit.*
HECTOR
    Now, youthful Troilus, do not these high strains
    Of divination in our sister work   114
    Some touches of remorse? Or is your blood   115
    So madly hot that no discourse of reason,
    Nor fear of bad success in a bad cause,
    Can qualify the same?   118
TROILUS   Why, brother Hector,
    We may not think the justness of each act   119
    Such and no other than event doth form it,   *120*
    Nor once deject the courage of our minds
    Because Cassandra's mad. Her brainsick raptures   122
    Cannot distaste the goodness of a quarrel   123
    Which hath our several honors all engaged   124
    To make it gracious. For my private part,   125
    I am no more touched than all Priam's sons;   126

---

106 *betimes* in advance   107 *moiety* part   108 *Practice* exercise   114 *div-ination* prophecy   115 *remorse* regret, compunction   118 *qualify* moderate   119–20 *We may not think . . . form it* we must not suppose that only out-comes justify particular actions   122 *raptures* prophetic ecstasies   123 *dis-taste* render distasteful   124 *several* separate   125 *gracious* worthy and admirable   126 *touched* affected

127 And Jove forbid there should be done amongst us
    Such things as might offend the weakest spleen
    To fight for and maintain.

PARIS
130 Else might the world convince of levity
    As well my undertakings as your counsels;
    But I attest the gods, your full consent
133 Gave wings to my propension and cut off
    All fears attending on so dire a project.
135 For what, alas, can these my single arms?
136 What propugnation is in one man's valor
137 To stand the push and enmity of those
138 This quarrel would excite? Yet, I protest,
139 Were I alone to pass the difficulties,
140 And had as ample power as I have will,
    Paris should ne'er retract what he hath done
142 Nor faint in the pursuit.

PRIAM   Paris, you speak
    Like one besotted on your sweet delights.
    You have the honey still, but these the gall;
    So to be valiant is no praise at all.

PARIS
    Sir, I propose not merely to myself
    The pleasures such a beauty brings with it;
148 But I would have the soil of her fair rape
    Wiped off in honorable keeping her.
150 What treason were it to the ransacked queen,
    Disgrace to your great worths, and shame to me,
    Now to deliver her possession up
153 On terms of base compulsion! Can it be
    That so degenerate a strain as this

127–29 *And Jove . . . maintain* God forbid that anything should be done to
upset the resolve of even the least courageous among us   130 *convince* con-
vict; *levity* frivolousness   133 *propension* inclination   135 *can* can accom-
plish   136 *propugnation* defense   137 *push* assault   138 *excite* inflame
139 *pass the difficulties* undergo the trials   142 *faint* flag   148 *soil* stain
150 *ransacked* abducted, stolen   153 *base compulsion* ignoble constraint

Should once set footing in your generous bosoms?   155
There's not the meanest spirit on our party
Without a heart to dare or sword to draw
When Helen is defended, nor none so noble
Whose life were ill bestowed or death unfamed   159
Where Helen is the subject. Then, I say,   160
Well may we fight for her whom, we know well,
The world's large spaces cannot parallel.

HECTOR
Paris and Troilus, you have both said well;
And on the cause and question now in hand
Have glozed – but superficially, not much   165
Unlike young men, whom Aristotle thought
Unfit to hear moral philosophy.   167
The reasons you allege do more conduce   168
To the hot passion of distempered blood   169
Than to make up a free determination   170
'Twixt right and wrong; for pleasure and revenge
Have ears more deaf than adders to the voice
Of any true decision. Nature craves
All dues be rendered to their owners. Now,
What nearer debt in all humanity
Than wife is to the husband? If this law
Of nature be corrupted through affection,   177
And that great minds, of partial indulgence   178
To their benumbèd wills, resist the same,   179
There is a law in each well-ordered nation   180
To curb those raging appetites that are
Most disobedient and refractory.
If Helen, then, be wife to Sparta's king,
As it is known she is, these moral laws

---

155 *generous* noble 159 *bestowed* expended 165 *glozed* commented,
glossed 167 *moral* (Aristotle wrote "political," but "moral" was often un-
derstood as well in Shakespeare's time) 168 *conduce* lead 169 *distempered*
intemperate, diseased 170 *free determination* impartial judgment 177 *affection* partiality, passion 178 *partial* self-serving 179 *benumbèd* i.e.,
oblivious of right and wrong

Of nature and of nations speak aloud
To have her back returned. Thus to persist
187   In doing wrong extenuates not wrong,
188   But makes it much more heavy. Hector's opinion
Is this in way of truth; yet ne'ertheless,
190   My spritely brethren, I propend to you
In resolution to keep Helen still;
For 'tis a cause that hath no mean dependence
193   Upon our joint and several dignities.

TROILUS
Why, there you touched the life of our design.
195   Were it not glory that we more affected
196   Than the performance of our heaving spleens,
I would not wish a drop of Trojan blood
Spent more in her defense. But, worthy Hector,
She is a theme of honor and renown,
200   A spur to valiant and magnanimous deeds,
Whose present courage may beat down our foes
202   And fame in time to come canonize us;
For I presume brave Hector would not lose
So rich advantage of a promised glory
As smiles upon the forehead of this action
For the wide world's revenue.

HECTOR   I am yours,
You valiant offspring of great Priamus.
208   I have a roisting challenge sent amongst
209   The dull and factious nobles of the Greeks
210   Will strike amazement to their drowsy spirits.
211   I was advertised their great general slept
212   Whilst emulation in the army crept.
This, I presume, will wake him.   *Exeunt.*

         *

---

187 *extenuates* lessens   188 *heavy* grave   190 *spritely* spirited; *propend* in-
cline   193 *joint and several* collective and individual   195 *affected* aspired to
196 *performance . . . spleens* acting on our aroused passions   202 *canonize*
immortalize as heroes   208 *roisting* rousing, boisterous   209 *factious* quar-
relsome, partisan   211 *advertised* informed   212 *emulation* envious rivalry

❧ **II.3** *Enter Thersites [alone].*

THERSITES How now, Thersites? What, lost in the
labyrinth of thy fury? Shall the elephant Ajax carry it   2
thus? He beats me, and I rail at him. O worthy satisfac-
tion! Would it were otherwise – that I could beat him,
whilst he railed at me. 'Sfoot, I'll learn to conjure and   5
raise devils, but I'll see some issue of my spiteful execra-   6
tions. Then there's Achilles, a rare engineer. If Troy be   7
not taken till these two undermine it, the walls will
stand till they fall of themselves. O thou great thunder
darter of Olympus, forget that thou art Jove, the king   10
of gods; and, Mercury, lose all the serpentine craft of
thy caduceus, if ye take not that little, little, less than   12
little wit from them that they have; which short-armed   13
ignorance itself knows is so abundant scarce it will not
in circumvention deliver a fly from a spider without   15
drawing their massy irons and cutting the web. After   16
this, the vengeance on the whole camp! Or, rather, the
Neapolitan boneache, for that, methinks, is the curse   18
depending on those that war for a placket. I have said   19
my prayers, and devil Envy say "Amen." What ho, my   20
Lord Achilles!
      Enter Patroclus.
PATROCLUS Who's there? Thersites? Good Thersites,
come in and rail.
THERSITES If I could 'a' remembered a gilt counterfeit,   24
thou wouldst not have slipped out of my contempla-

II.3 Before the tent of Achilles **2** *carry it* carry off the honors **5** *'Sfoot*
(contraction of "God's foot"); *conjure* invoke, summon up **6** *issue* outcome
7 *rare engineer* exceptional plotter **12** *caduceus* (Mercury's staff of office,
formed from two twining serpents) **13** *short-armed* lacking (intellectual)
reach **15** *in circumvention* in attempting to outwit **16** *massy irons* heavy
swords **18** *Neapolitan boneache* syphilis **19** *depending on* attendant upon;
placket petticoat (by implication, vagina) **24** *'a'* have; *gilt counterfeit* counterfeit coin of brass covered with gold, also known as a "slip" (by insinuation
here, a gelded, counterfeit male)

26 tion. But it is no matter. Thyself upon thyself! The
common curse of mankind, folly and ignorance, be
28 thine in great revenue. Heaven bless thee from a tutor,
29 and discipline come not near thee. Let thy blood be thy
30 direction till thy death. Then, if she that lays thee out
31 says thou art a fair corse, I'll be sworn and sworn upon't
32 she never shrouded any but lazars. Amen. Where's
Achilles?

PATROCLUS What, art thou devout? Wast thou in
prayer?

THERSITES Ay; the heavens hear me!

PATROCLUS Amen.
          Enter Achilles.

ACHILLES Who's there?

PATROCLUS Thersites, my lord.

40 ACHILLES Where, where, O, where? Art thou come?
41 Why, my cheese, my digestion, why hast thou not
served thyself in to my table so many meals? Come,
what's Agamemnon?

THERSITES Thy commander, Achilles. Then tell me, Patroclus, what's Achilles?

PATROCLUS Thy lord, Thersites. Then tell me, I pray
thee, what's thyself?

THERSITES Thy knower, Patroclus. Then tell me, Patroclus, what art thou?

50 PATROCLUS Thou must tell that knowest.

ACHILLES O tell, tell.

52 THERSITES I'll decline the whole question. Agamemnon
commands Achilles, Achilles is my lord, I am Patroclus'
knower, and Patroclus is a fool.

[PATROCLUS You rascal!

THERSITES Peace, fool! I have not done.

---

26 *Thyself upon thyself* i.e., be what you are – nothing could be worse for you
28 *revenue* abundance; *bless thee from* save you from (i.e., keep you as igno-
rant as you are)   29–30 *Let thy blood . . . direction* may your passions guide
you   31 *corse* corpse   32 *lazars* lepers   41 *digestion* digestive snack   52 *decline* go through (as in declining a noun)

ACHILLES   He is a privileged man. Proceed, Thersites.   57

THERSITES   Agamemnon is a fool, Achilles is a fool,
Thersites is a fool, and, as aforesaid, Patroclus is a fool.]

ACHILLES   Derive this. Come!   60

THERSITES   Agamemnon is a fool to offer to command
Achilles, Achilles is a fool to be commanded of
Agamemnon, Thersites is a fool to serve such a fool,
and this Patroclus is a fool positive.   64

PATROCLUS   Why am I a fool?

THERSITES   Make that demand to the creator; it suffices
me thou art. Look you, who comes here?

Enter [at a distance] Agamemnon, Ulysses, Nestor,
Diomedes, Ajax, and Calchas.

ACHILLES   Come, Patroclus, I'll speak with nobody.
Come in with me, Thersites.   *Exit.*

THERSITES   Here is such patchery, such juggling, and   70
such knavery. All the argument is a whore and a cuck-   71
old, a good quarrel to draw emulous factions and bleed   72
to death upon. [Now, the dry serpigo on the subject,   73
and war and lechery confound all!]   *[Exit.]*

AGAMEMNON   Where is Achilles?

PATROCLUS
Within his tent, but ill-disposed, my lord.

AGAMEMNON
Let it be known to him that we are here.
He shent our messengers, and we lay by   78
Our appertainings, visiting of him.   79
Let him be told so, lest perchance he think   80
We dare not move the question of our place   81
Or know not what we are.

PATROCLUS   I shall so say to him. *[Exit.]*

---

57 *privileged man* i.e., a licensed fool   60 *Derive* expound   64 *positive* ab-
solutely   70 *patchery* roguery; *juggling* trickery   71 *argument* cause of contention   72 *emulous factions* envious rival parties   73 *serpigo* skin eruption;
subject topic   78 *shent* reviled   79 *appertainings* prerogatives of kingly rank
81 *move the question . . . place* raise the issue of my superior rank

ULYSSES   We saw him at the opening of his tent. He is
not sick.

AJAX   Yes, lion-sick, sick of proud heart. You may call it
melancholy if you will favor the man, but, by my head,
'tis pride. But why, why? Let him show us a cause. [A
word, my lord.]
    [Takes Agamemnon aside.]

NESTOR   What moves Ajax thus to bay at him?

90   ULYSSES   Achilles hath inveigled his fool from him.

NESTOR   Who, Thersites?

ULYSSES   He.

NESTOR   Then will Ajax lack matter, if he have lost his
94   argument.

95   ULYSSES   No, you see, he is his argument that has his argument: Achilles.

97   NESTOR   All the better; their fraction is more our wish
98   than their faction. But it was a strong composure a fool
could disunite.

100   ULYSSES   The amity that wisdom knits not, folly may easily untie.
    [Enter Patroclus.]
Here comes Patroclus.

NESTOR   No Achilles with him?

ULYSSES
104   The elephant hath joints, but none for courtesy.
105   His legs are legs for necessity, not for flexure.

PATROCLUS
Achilles bids me say he is much sorry
If anything more than your sport and pleasure
108   Did move your greatness and this noble state
To call upon him. He hopes it is no other
110   But, for your health and your digestion sake,

---

90 *inveigled* enticed, seduced 94 *argument* i.e., the subject of his verbal
abuse 95–96 *he is . . . his argument* i.e., Achilles has become Ajax's argument by stealing his argument 97 *fraction* discord 98 *faction* alliance;
composure bond 104 *courtesy* kneeling deferentially 105 *flexure* bending
108 *state* retinue, assembly

An after-dinner's breath.   111
AGAMEMNON   Hear you, Patroclus:
  We are too well acquainted with these answers;
  But his evasion, winged thus swift with scorn,
  Cannot outfly our apprehensions.   114
  Much attribute he hath, and much the reason   115
  Why we ascribe it to him; yet all his virtues,
  Not virtuously on his own part beheld,   117
  Do in our eyes begin to lose their gloss,
  Yea, like fair fruit in an unwholesome dish,
  Are like to rot untasted. Go and tell him,   120
  We come to speak with him; and you shall not sin
  If you do say we think him over-proud
  And under-honest, in self-assumption greater   123
  Than in the note of judgment; and worthier than him-   124
    self
  Here tend the savage strangeness he puts on,   125
  Disguise the holy strength of their command,   126
  And underwrite in an observing kind   127
  His humorous predominance; yea, watch   128
  His course and time, his ebbs and flows, as if
  The passage and whole carriage of this action   130
  Rode on his tide. Go tell him this, and add
  That, if he overhold his price so much,   132
  We'll none of him, but let him, like an engine   133
  Not portable, lie under this report:
  "Bring action hither, this cannot go to war."
  A stirring dwarf we do allowance give   136

---

111 *breath* stroll   114 *outfly . . . apprehensions* (1) outrun our arrest, (2) escape our understanding   115 *attribute* reputation   117 *beheld* maintained   123 *self-assumption* arrogant self-regard   124 *note of judgment* view of the judicious   125 *tend* attend; *savage strangeness* rude aloofness   126 *Disguise . . . command* veil the rightful authority they (could) wield   127 *underwrite . . . observing kind* submit in deferential fashion   128 *humorous predominance* (1) capricious domination, (2) rule of humors over reason in him   130 *carriage* conduct   132 *overhold* overestimate   133 *engine* mechanical device used in war (e.g., cannon)   136 *stirring* wakeful, active; *allowance* credit

Before a sleeping giant. Tell him so.

PATROCLUS
    I shall, and bring his answer presently.   *[Exit.]*

AGAMEMNON
139   In second voice we'll not be satisfied;
140   We come to speak with him. Ulysses, enter you.
                               [Exit Ulysses.]

AJAX   What is he more than another?

AGAMEMNON   No more than what he thinks he is.

AJAX   Is he so much? Do you not think he thinks himself
a better man than I am?

AGAMEMNON   No question.

146 AJAX   Will you subscribe his thought, and say he is?

AGAMEMNON   No, noble Ajax. You are as strong, as
148   valiant, as wise, no less noble, much more gentle, and
149   altogether more tractable.

150 AJAX   Why should a man be proud? How doth pride
grow? I know not what pride is.

AGAMEMNON   Your mind is the clearer and your virtues
the fairer. He that is proud eats up himself. Pride is his
154   own glass, his own trumpet, his own chronicle; and
155   whatever praises itself but in the deed, devours the deed
in the praise.

AJAX   I do hate a proud man, as I do hate the engender-
ing of toads.

NESTOR   *[Aside]* And yet he loves himself. Is't not strange?
    Enter Ulysses.

ULYSSES
160   Achilles will not to the field tomorrow.

AGAMEMNON
    What's his excuse?

ULYSSES   He doth rely on none,
162   But carries on the stream of his dispose

---

139 *second voice* spokesperson, delegate   146 *subscribe* endorse   148 *gentle*
well-bred   149 *tractable* amenable   154 *glass* mirror; *trumpet* trumpeter;
chronicle historical record   155 *but in the deed* except in action   162 *carries . . . dispose* rides on the current of his inclination

Without observance or respect of any,   163
In will peculiar and in self-admission.   164
AGAMEMNON
Why will he not upon our fair request
Untent his person and share the air with us?
ULYSSES
Things small as nothing, for request's sake only,   167
He makes important. Possessed he is with greatness,   168
And speaks not to himself but with a pride   169
That quarrels at self-breath. Imagined worth   170
Holds in his blood such swoll'n and hot discourse   171
That 'twixt his mental and his active parts
Kingdomed Achilles in commotion rages   173
And batters down himself. What should I say?
He is so plaguy proud that the death tokens of it   175
Cry "No recovery."
AGAMEMNON   Let Ajax go to him.
Dear lord, go you and greet him in his tent.
'Tis said he holds you well, and will be led   178
At your request a little from himself.   179
ULYSSES
O Agamemnon, let it not be so!   180
We'll consecrate the steps that Ajax makes   181
When they go from Achilles. Shall the proud lord
That bastes his arrogance with his own seam   183
And never suffers matter of the world
Enter his thoughts, save such as doth revolve   185
And ruminate himself – shall he be worshiped
Of that we hold an idol more than he?   187

---

163 *observance* regard   **164** *In will . . . self-admission* i.e., relying on his own
will and self-approval   **167** *for . . . only* merely because they are requested
168 *Possessed* captivated   **169–70** *speaks . . . self-breath* i.e., he is so proud
that he balks at speaking even to himself   **171** *swol'n and hot discourse* in-
flated and passionate urging   **173** *Kingdomed* i.e., like a kingdom (experiencing civil war)   **175** *death tokens* signs of impending death   **178** *holds*
regards   **179** *from himself* out of his normal behavior   **181–82** *We'll . . .
Achilles* i.e., we'll honor Ajax for departing from Achilles rather than for approaching him   **183** *seam* grease   **185–86** *revolve / And ruminate* concern
and reflect upon   **187** *idol* heroic image

No, this thrice-worthy and right valiant lord
189 Shall not so stale his palm, nobly acquired,
190 Nor, by my will, assubjugate his merit,
191 As amply titled as Achilles' is,
By going to Achilles.
193 That were to enlard his fat-already pride,
194 And add more coals to Cancer when he burns
195 With entertaining great Hyperion.
This lord go to him! Jupiter forbid,
And say in thunder, "Achilles, go to him."

NESTOR *[Aside]*
198 O, this is well. He rubs the vein of him.

DIOMEDES *[Aside]*
And how his silence drinks up his applause!

AJAX
200 If I go to him, with my armèd fist
201 I'll pash him o'er the face.

AGAMEMNON
O, no, you shall not go.

AJAX
203 An he be proud with me, I'll pheese his pride.
Let me go to him.

ULYSSES
Not for the worth that hangs upon our quarrel.

AJAX A paltry, insolent fellow!

NESTOR *[Aside]* How he describes himself!

AJAX Can he not be sociable?

ULYSSES *[Aside]* The raven chides blackness.

210 AJAX I'll let his humorous blood.

AGAMEMNON *[Aside]* He will be the physician that
should be the patient.

213 AJAX An all men were of my mind –

---

189 *stale his palm* debase his crown of glory 190 *assubjugate* subordinate
191 *amply titled* (1) well earned, (2) nobly founded 193 *enlard* smear with
(more) fat 194 *Cancer* i.e., summer, which begins under this sign of the zodiac 195 *Hyperion* the sun 198 *rubs the vein* indulges (massages) his disposition 201 *pash* beat, hit 203 *An* if; *pheese* settle the matter of 210
let . . . blood cure his humoral disease by letting blood 213 *An* if only

ULYSSES   *[Aside]* Wit would be out of fashion.
AJAX   – a should not bear it so, a should eat swords first.   215
  Shall pride carry it?   216
NESTOR   *[Aside]* An 'twould, you'd carry half.
ULYSSES   *[Aside]* A would have ten shares.
AJAX   I will knead him; I'll make him supple.
NESTOR   *[Aside]* He's not yet through warm. Force him   220
  with praises; pour in, pour in; his ambition is dry.
ULYSSES   *[To Agamemnon]*
  My lord, you feed too much on this dislike.
NESTOR
  Our noble general, do not do so.
DIOMEDES
  You must prepare to fight without Achilles.
ULYSSES
  Why, 'tis this naming of him does him harm.
  Here is a man – but 'tis before his face;
  I will be silent.
NESTOR   Wherefore should you so?
  He is not emulous, as Achilles is.   228
ULYSSES
  Know the whole world, he is as valiant –
AJAX
  A whoreson dog, that shall palter with us thus!   230
  Would he were a Trojan!
NESTOR   What a vice were it in Ajax now –
ULYSSES   If he were proud –
DIOMEDES   Or covetous of praise –
ULYSSES   Ay, or surly borne –   235
DIOMEDES   Or strange, or self-affected!   236
ULYSSES   *[To Ajax]*
  Thank the heavens, lord, thou art of sweet composure;   237
  Praise him that got thee, she that gave thee suck;   238

---

215 *a* he   216 *carry it* prevail   220 *through* thoroughly   228 *emulous* enviously conceited   230 *whoreson* bastard; *palter* trifle   235 *borne* in bearing
236 *strange* proudly aloof; *self-affected* conceited   237 *composure* composi-
tion   238 *got* begot

239 Famed be thy tutor, and thy parts of nature
240 Thrice-famed beyond all erudition;
241 But he that disciplined thine arms to fight,
242 Let Mars divide eternity in twain
     And give him half; and, for thy vigor,
244 Bull-bearing Milo his addition yield
245 To sinewy Ajax. I will not praise thy wisdom,
246 Which, like a bourn, a pale, a shore, confines
247 Thy spacious and dilated parts. Here's Nestor,
248 Instructed by the antiquary times,
     He must, he is, he cannot but be wise.
250 But pardon, father Nestor, were your days
251 As green as Ajax, and your brain so tempered,
252 You should not have the eminence of him,
     But be as Ajax.

AJAX   Shall I call you father?

NESTOR

254 Ay, my good son.

DIOMEDES   Be ruled by him, Lord Ajax.

ULYSSES

255 There is no tarrying here; the hart Achilles
256 Keeps thicket. Please it our great general
257 To call together all his state of war.
     Fresh kings are come to Troy. Tomorrow,
259 We must with all our main of power stand fast.
260 And here's a lord – come knights from east to west,
261 And cull their flower, Ajax shall cope the best.

AGAMEMNON

     Go we to council. Let Achilles sleep:

---

239 *parts of nature* natural endowments   241 *disciplined* trained   242 *divide eternity in twain* divide his immortality in half   244 *Bull-bearing Milo* famously strong Greek athlete; *addition* honorific title   245 *sinewy* muscular   246 *bourn* boundary; *pale* containing fence   247 *dilated parts* extensive abilities   248 *antiquary* ancient   251 *green* youthful; *tempered* well-conditioned   252 *have the eminence of* take precedence over   254 *Be ruled by* take advice from   255 *hart* male deer   256 *Keeps thicket* remains hidden in the brush   257 *state of war* military council   259 *main of power* military might   261 *cull their flower* pick out their best warriors; *cope* contend with

Light boats sail swift, though greater hulks draw deep.   263
                                                 Exeunt.

                            *

✢ **III.1** *[Music sounds within.] Enter Pandarus [and a
    Servant].*

PANDARUS   Friend you, pray you a word. Do you not fol-   1
    low the young Lord Paris?
SERVANT   Ay, sir, when he goes before me.
PANDARUS   You depend upon him, I mean.   4
SERVANT   Sir, I do depend upon the Lord.
PANDARUS   You depend upon a noble gentleman; I must
    needs praise him.
SERVANT   The Lord be praised!
PANDARUS   You know me, do you not?
SERVANT   Faith, sir, superficially.   10
PANDARUS   Friend, know me better. I am the Lord Pan-
    darus.
SERVANT   I hope I shall know your honor better.
PANDARUS   I do desire it.
SERVANT   You are in the state of grace?   15
PANDARUS   Grace? Not so, friend. Honor and lordship   16
    are my titles. What music is this?
SERVANT   I do but partly know, sir. It is music in parts. 18
PANDARUS   Know you the musicians?
SERVANT   Wholly, sir.   20
PANDARUS   Who play they to?
SERVANT   To the hearers, sir.
PANDARUS   At whose pleasure, friend?
SERVANT   At mine, sir, and theirs that love music.
PANDARUS   Command, I mean, friend.
SERVANT   Who shall I command, sir?

---

263 *hulks* large, bulky vessels
    III.1 Priam's palace   **1–2** *follow* wait upon   **4** *depend upon him* are a de-
pendent of his   **15** *You . . . grace* i.e., because you wish to know better   **16**
Grace (title of address to a duke)   **18** *in parts* divided into parts

PANDARUS   Friend, we understand not one another. I am
too courtly, and thou too cunning. At whose request do
these men play?

30   SERVANT   That's to't, indeed, sir. Marry, sir, at the request
of Paris, my lord, who is there in person; with him the
mortal Venus, the heartblood of beauty, love's invisible
soul.

PANDARUS   Who? My cousin Cressida?

SERVANT   No, sir, Helen. Could you not find out that by
her attributes?

PANDARUS   It should seem, fellow, that thou hast not
seen the Lady Cressid. I come to speak with Paris from
the Prince Troilus. I will make a complimental assault

40   upon him, for my business seethes.

41   SERVANT   Sodden business! There's a stewed phrase, indeed.

     Enter Paris and Helen [with Musicians].

43   PANDARUS   Fair be to you, my lord, and to all this fair
company. Fair desires in all fair measure fairly guide

45   them, especially to you, fair queen. Fair thoughts be
your fair pillow.

HELEN   Dear lord, you are full of fair words.

PANDARUS   You speak your fair pleasure, sweet queen.

49   Fair prince, here is good broken music.

50   PARIS   You have broke it, cousin; and, by my life, you

51   shall make it whole again; you shall piece it out with a
piece of your performance. Nell, he is full of harmony.

PANDARUS   Truly, lady, no.

HELEN   O, sir!

55   PANDARUS   Rude, in sooth; in good sooth, very rude.

56   PARIS   Well said, my lord. Well, you say so in fits.

---

30 *to't* to the point   40 *seethes* is urgent   41 *Sodden* boiled; *stewed* (punning
on "stew," brothel)   43 *Fair be* good wishes   45 *queen* (with possible pun
on "quean," slut)   49 *broken* divided for different groups of instruments
(e.g., strings and winds)   50 *broke* interrupted   51 *piece it out* repair or elaborate it   55 *Rude* untrained, incapable   56 *fits* repeated phrases, parts of a
song

PANDARUS I have business to my lord, dear queen. My
lord, will you vouchsafe me a word?   58

HELEN Nay, this shall not hedge us out. We'll hear you   59
sing, certainly.   60

PANDARUS Well, sweet queen, you are pleasant with me.   61
But, marry, thus, my lord: my dear lord and most es-
teemed friend, your brother Troilus –

HELEN My Lord Pandarus, honey-sweet lord –

PANDARUS Go to, sweet queen, go to – commends him-   65
self most affectionately to you.

HELEN You shall not bob us out of our melody. If you   67
do, our melancholy upon your head!

PANDARUS Sweet queen, sweet queen; that's a sweet
queen, i' faith –   70

HELEN And to make a sweet lady sad is a sour offense.

PANDARUS Nay, that shall not serve your turn; that shall
it not, in truth, la. Nay, I care not for such words; no,   73
no. And, my lord, he desires you that, if the king call
for him at supper, you will make his excuse.

HELEN My Lord Pandarus –

PANDARUS What says my sweet queen, my very, very
sweet queen?

PARIS What exploit's in hand? Where sups he tonight?   79

HELEN Nay, but my lord –   80

PANDARUS What says my sweet queen? My cousin will
fall out with you.

HELEN *[To Paris]* You must not know where he sups.

PARIS I'll lay my life, with my disposer Cressida.   84

PANDARUS No, no; no such matter; you are wide. Come,   85
your disposer is sick.

PARIS Well, I'll make excuse.

PANDARUS Ay, good my lord. Why should you say Cressida? No, your poor disposer's sick.

---

58 *vouchsafe* grant **59** *hedge us out* thwart us **61** *pleasant* humorous **65**
Go to leave off **67** *bob* cheat **73** *la* (term of emphasis) **79** *in hand* in the
making **84** *disposer* i.e., the one who manages me **85** *wide* wide of the
mark

90 PARIS   I spy.

PANDARUS   You spy? What do you spy? Come, give me
an instrument now, sweet queen.

HELEN   Why, this is kindly done.

94 PANDARUS   My niece is horribly in love with a thing you
have, sweet queen.

HELEN   She shall have it, my lord, if it be not my Lord
Paris.

PANDARUS   He? No, she'll none of him; they two are
99 twain.

100 HELEN   Falling in after falling out may make them three.

PANDARUS   Come, come, I'll hear no more of this. I'll
sing you a song now.

103 HELEN   Ay, ay, prithee. Now by my troth, sweet lord,
thou hast a fine forehead.

105 PANDARUS   Ay, you may, you may.

HELEN   Let thy song be love. This love will undo us all.
O Cupid, Cupid, Cupid!

PANDARUS   Love! ay, that it shall, i' faith.

109 PARIS   Ay, good, now "Love, love, nothing but love."

110 PANDARUS   [In good troth, it begins so:]
[Sings.]
Love, love, nothing but love, still love still more!
For, O, love's bow shoots buck and doe.
113 The shaft confounds not that it wounds,
114 But tickles still the sore.
115 These lovers cry, O ho! they die!
Yet that which seems the wound to kill
117 Doth turn O ho! to Ha, ha, he!
So dying love lives still.

94–95 *thing you have* (implying the penis Helen already enjoys in her relationship with Paris)   99 *twain* at odds   103 *prithee* I pray you (conven-
tional courtesy)   105 *you may* i.e., you may joke on   109 *good, now* if you
please   113 *confounds* injures   114 *sore* buck in its fourth year (implying the
"wound" of women's sexual anatomy)   115 *die* (colloquial term for orgasm)
117 *O ho* (exclamation of pain); *Ha, ha, he* (cries of sexual pleasure)

O ho! a while, but Ha, ha, ha!

O ho! groans out for Ha, ha, ha! – Heigh ho!   120

HELEN   In love, i' faith, to the very tip of the nose.

PARIS   He eats nothing but doves, love, and that breeds   122
hot blood, and hot blood begets hot thoughts, and hot
thoughts beget hot deeds, and hot deeds is love.

PANDARUS   Is this the generation of love: hot blood, hot   125
thoughts, and hot deeds? Why, they are vipers. Is love a
generation of vipers? Sweet lord, who's afield today?

PARIS   Hector, Deiphobus, Helenus, Antenor, and all the
gallantry of Troy. I would fain have armed today, but   129
my Nell would not have it so. How chance my brother   130
Troilus went not?

HELEN   He hangs the lip at something. You know all,   132
Lord Pandarus.

PANDARUS   Not I, honey-sweet queen. I long to hear
how they sped today. You'll remember your brother's   135
excuse?

PARIS   To a hair.

PANDARUS   Farewell, sweet queen.

HELEN   Commend me to your niece.

PANDARUS   I will, sweet queen.   *[Exit.] Sound a retreat.*   140

PARIS

They're come from the field. Let us to Priam's hall
To greet the warriors. Sweet Helen, I must woo you
To help unarm our Hector. His stubborn buckles,
With these your white enchanting fingers touched,
Shall more obey than to the edge of steel
Or force of Greekish sinews. You shall do more
Than all the island kings: disarm great Hector.   147

HELEN

'Twill make us proud to be his servant, Paris.
Yea, what he shall receive of us in duty

---

120 *groans out for* i.e., exclamations of pain are really expressions of desire
122 *doves* (often associated with Venus)   125 *generation* lineage   129 *gallantry* gallants; *would fain* wanted to (perhaps with a pun on "feign," pretend)   132 *hangs the lip* pouts   135 *sped* fared   147 *island* i.e., Greek

150   Gives us more palm in beauty than we have,
    Yea, overshines ourself.

PARIS
    Sweet, above thought I love thee.   *Exeunt.*

            *

∽ **III.2** *Enter Pandarus [and] Troilus' Boy.*

PANDARUS   How now, where's thy master? At my cousin
    Cressida's?
BOY   No, sir; he stays for you to conduct him thither.
    [Enter Troilus.]
PANDARUS   O, here he comes. How now, how now?
5 TROILUS   Sirrah, walk off.   *[Exit Boy.]*
PANDARUS   Have you seen my cousin?
TROILUS
    No, Pandarus. I stalk about her door
8   Like a strange soul upon the Stygian banks
9   Staying for waftage. O, be thou my Charon,
10   And give me swift transportance to those fields
    Where I may wallow in the lily beds
12   Proposed for the deserver. O gentle Pandar,
    From Cupid's shoulder pluck his painted wings,
    And fly with me to Cressid.
PANDARUS
15   Walk here i' th' orchard. I'll bring her straight. *[Exit.]*
TROILUS
    I am giddy; expectation whirls me round.
    Th' imaginary relish is so sweet
    That it enchants my sense. What will it be
19   When that the wat'ry palates taste indeed

---

150 *palm in* honor for
    III.2 Pandarus's garden   **5** *Sirrah* (form of address to a social inferior)   **8**
Stygian (pertaining to the river Styx, crossed by the spirits of the dead enter-
ing the afterlife in Greek mythology)   **9** *waftage* conveyance by boat;
Charon ferryman across the Styx   **12** *Proposed for* promised to   **15** *orchard*
garden   **19** *wat'ry* (1) accustomed to water, (2) watering in anticipation

Love's thrice-repurèd nectar? Death, I fear me,   20
Sounding destruction, or some joy too fine,   21
Too subtle, potent, tuned too sharp in sweetness
For the capacity of my ruder powers.
I fear it much; and I do fear besides
That I shall lose distinction in my joys,   25
As doth a battle, when they charge on heaps   26
The enemy flying.
        [Enter Pandarus.]
PANDARUS   She's making her ready; she'll come straight.
You must be witty now. She does so blush, and fetches   29
her wind so short as if she were frayed with a spirit. I'll   30
fetch her. It is the prettiest villain; she fetches her   31
breath as short as a new-ta'en sparrow.   *[Exit.]*   32
TROILUS
Even such a passion doth embrace my bosom.
My heart beats thicker than a feverous pulse,
And all my powers do their bestowing lose,   35
Like vassalage at unawares encount'ring   36
The eye of majesty.
        Enter Pandarus and Cressida [veiled].
PANDARUS   Come, come, what need you blush? Shame's
a baby. Here she is now; swear the oaths now to her
that you have sworn to me. *[To Cressida]* What! are you   40
gone again? You must be watched ere you be made   41
tame, must you? Come your ways, come your ways; an   42
you draw backward, we'll put you i' th' fills. *[To Troilus]*   43
Why do you not speak to her? *[To Cressida]* Come,
draw this curtain, and let's see your picture. Alas the   45
day, how loath you are to offend daylight! An 'twere   46

---

20 *thrice-repurèd* triply distilled   21 *Sounding* swooning   25 *distinction* the
power to distinguish   26 *battle* army; *on heaps* in a mass   29 *be witty* have
your wits about you   29–30 *fetches . . . short* pants   30 *frayed with a spirit*
frightened by a ghost   31 *villain* miscreant (here used as a term of endear-
ment)   32 *new-ta'en* newly caught   35 *bestowing* proper use   36 *vassalage*
vassals   41 *watched* kept awake (method used in hawk taming)   42 *Come
your ways* come along; *an* if   43 *fills* shafts (of a cart)   45 *curtain* i.e., veil;
picture image (i.e., face)   46 *An 'twere* if it were

47   dark, you'd close sooner. *[To Troilus]* So, so; rub on, and
48   kiss the mistress. *[They kiss.]* How now, a kiss in fee
      farm! Build there, carpenter; the air is sweet. Nay, you
50   shall fight your hearts out ere I part you. The falcon as
51   the tercel, for all the ducks i' th' river. Go to, go to.

TROILUS   You have bereft me of all words, lady.

PANDARUS   Words pay no debts, give her deeds. But
54   she'll bereave you o' th' deeds too if she call your activ-
55   ity in question. *[They kiss.]* What, billing again? Here's
56   "In witness whereof the parties interchangeably." Come
      in, come in. I'll go get a fire.   *[Exit.]*

CRESSIDA   Will you walk in, my lord?

TROILUS   O Cressid, how often have I wished me thus!

60 CRESSIDA   Wished, my lord? The gods grant – O my lord!

TROILUS   What should they grant? What makes this
62   pretty abruption? What too-curious dreg espies my
      sweet lady in the fountain of our love?

CRESSIDA   More dregs than water, if my fears have eyes.

65 TROILUS   Fears make devils of cherubins; they never see
      truly.

CRESSIDA   Blind fear, that seeing reason leads, finds safer
      footing than blind reason stumbling without fear. To
      fear the worst oft cures the worse.

70 TROILUS   O, let my lady apprehend no fear. In all
71   Cupid's pageant there is presented no monster.

CRESSIDA   Nor nothing monstrous neither?

---

47 *close* unite, come to grips   47–48 *rub on . . . mistress* i.e., overcome the obstacles and reach the object (expression from the game of bowls, where *rubs* are
obstacles, and balls that touch one another are said to *kiss*)   48–49 *fee farm*
i.e., perpetuity (derived from perpetual land tenure at a fixed rent)   50–51
The falcon . . . tercel i.e., I'll bet the *falcon* (female hawk, Cressida) will match
the male hawk (*tercel*, Troilus) in the "devouring" sport of love   51 *all the
ducks i' th' river* i.e., the stake in the bet or the prey to be devoured; *Go to* get
on with it   54 *bereave you o' th' deeds* undo your sexual potency   54–55 *activity* sexual prowess   55 *billing* kissing   56 *In witness . . . interchangeably* (legal
formula of agreement, completed by the words "have set their hands and
seals")   62 *abruption* breaking off; *too-curious dreg* anxiety-producing sediment   65 *Fears . . . cherubins* terrors make angels look like devils   71 *pageant*
stage tableau

TROILUS   Nothing but our undertakings when we vow to weep seas, live in fire, eat rocks, tame tigers, thinking it harder for our mistress to devise imposition enough than for us to undergo any difficulty imposed. This is the monstruosity in love, lady, that the will is infinite 77 and the execution confined; that the desire is boundless and the act a slave to limit.

CRESSIDA   They say all lovers swear more performance 80 than they are able, and yet reserve an ability that they never perform, vowing more than the perfection of ten and discharging less than the tenth part of one. They that have the voice of lions and the act of hares, are they not monsters?

TROILUS   Are there such? Such are not we. Praise us as we are tasted, allow us as we prove; our head shall go bare 87 till merit crown it. No perfection in reversion shall have 88 a praise in present; we will not name desert before his 89 birth, and, being born, his addition shall be humble. 90 Few words to fair faith. Troilus shall be such to Cressid, as what envy can say worst shall be a mock for his 92 truth, and what truth can speak truest not truer than Troilus.

CRESSIDA   Will you walk in, my lord?
    [Enter Pandarus.]

PANDARUS   What, blushing still? Have you not done talking yet?

CRESSIDA   Well, uncle, what folly I commit, I dedicate to you.

PANDARUS   I thank you for that. If my lord get a boy of 100 you, you'll give him me. Be true to my lord; if he flinch, chide me for it.

TROILUS   *[To Cressida]* You know now your hostages, 103 your uncle's word and my firm faith.

---

77 *monstruosity* monstrousness   87 *tasted* put to the test; *allow* approve   88 *reversion* right of future possession   89 *desert* deserving   90 *addition* title of honor   92–94 *as what . . . Troilus* that malice itself can do no more than sneer at Troilus for his constancy   103 *hostages* guarantees

PANDARUS   Nay, I'll give my word for her too. Our kin-
dred, though they be long ere they be wooed, they are
constant being won. They are burrs, I can tell you;
they'll stick where they are thrown.

CRESSIDA
Boldness comes to me now and brings me heart.
110   Prince Troilus, I have loved you night and day
For many weary months.

TROILUS
Why was my Cressid then so hard to win?

CRESSIDA
Hard to seem won; but I was won, my lord,
With the first glance that ever — pardon me:
If I confess much you will play the tyrant.
I love you now, but not, till now, so much
But I might master it. In faith, I lie;
118   My thoughts were like unbridled children grown
Too headstrong for their mother. See, we fools!
120   Why have I blabbed? Who shall be true to us
When we are so unsecret to ourselves?
But, though I loved you well, I wooed you not;
And yet, good faith, I wished myself a man,
Or that we women had men's privilege
Of speaking first. Sweet, bid me hold my tongue,
For in this rapture I shall surely speak
The thing I shall repent. See, see! your silence,
Cunning in dumbness, for my weakness draws
129   My very soul of counsel. Stop my mouth.

TROILUS
130   And shall, albeit sweet music issues thence. *[Kisses her.]*
PANDARUS   Pretty, i' faith.
CRESSIDA   *[To Troilus]*
My lord, I do beseech you, pardon me;
'Twas not my purpose thus to beg a kiss.
I am ashamed. O heavens, what have I done?
For this time will I take my leave, my lord.

---

118 *unbridled* undisciplined   129 *My . . . counsel* my inmost secrets

TROILUS
   Your leave, sweet Cressid?

PANDARUS   Leave! An you take leave till tomorrow   137
   morning –

CRESSIDA
   Pray you, content you.

TROILUS   What offends you, lady?

CRESSIDA
   Sir, mine own company.   *140*

TROILUS
   You cannot shun yourself.

CRESSIDA
   Let me go and try.
   I have a kind of self resides with you;
   But an unkind self, that itself will leave   144
   To be another's fool. I would be gone.   145
   Where is my wit? I know not what I speak.

TROILUS
   Well know they what they speak that speak so wisely.

CRESSIDA
   Perchance, my lord, I show more craft than love,
   And fell so roundly to a large confession   149
   To angle for your thoughts. But you are wise,   150
   Or else you love not, for to be wise and love
   Exceeds man's might; that dwells with gods above.

TROILUS
   O! that I thought it could be in a woman –
   As, if it can, I will presume in you –
   To feed for aye her lamp and flames of love;   155
   To keep her constancy in plight and youth,   156
   Outliving beauty's outward, with a mind   157
   That doth renew swifter than blood decays;
   Or that persuasion could but thus convince me
   That my integrity and truth to you   *160*

---

137 *An* if   144 *unkind* cruel, unnatural   145 *fool* dupe   149 *roundly*
frankly   150 *angle* fish   155 *for aye* forever   156 *in plight and youth* as fresh
and constant as when it was plighted   157 *outward* superficial appearance

161   Might be affronted with the match and weight
      Of such a winnowed purity in love;
      How were I then uplifted! But, alas,
      I am as true as truth's simplicity,
165   And simpler than the infancy of truth.

CRESSIDA

166   In that I'll war with you.

TROILUS   O virtuous fight,
      When right with right wars who shall be most right!
168   True swains in love shall in the world to come
169   Approve their truth by Troilus. When their rhymes,
170   Full of protest, of oath, and big compare,
171   Wants similes, truth tired with iteration,
172   "As true as steel, as plantage to the moon,
173   As sun to day, as turtle to her mate,
174   As iron to adamant, as earth to th' center,"
      Yet, after all comparisons of truth,
176   As truth's authentic author to be cited,
      "As true as Troilus" shall crown up the verse
178   And sanctify the numbers.

CRESSIDA   Prophet may you be!
      If I be false or swerve a hair from truth,
180   When time is old and hath forgot itself,
      When waterdrops have worn the stones of Troy,
      And blind oblivion swallowed cities up,
183   And mighty states characterless are grated
      To dusty nothing, yet let memory,
185   From false to false among false maids in love,
      Upbraid my falsehood! When th' have said, "As false

---

161 *affronted* matched   161–62 *match and weight . . . in love* equal quantity and weight of pure love winnowed from the chaff   165 *the infancy of truth* i.e., (1) before it encountered falsehood, (2) as infants are true   166 *war* compete   168 *swains* lovers   169 *Approve* attest, verify   170 *big compare* hyperbole   171 *Wants* lacks; *iteration* repetition   172 *plantage* vegetation (supposedly influenced by the *moon*)   173 *turtle* turtledove   174 *adamant* a magnetic lodestone; *center* center of the earth as the supposed point of attraction   176 *authentic . . . cited* genuine authority or source to be quoted   178 *numbers* verse lines   183 *characterless* leaving no record   185 *false to false* false one to false one

As air, as water, wind or sandy earth,
As fox to lamb, as wolf to heifer's calf,
Pard to the hind, or stepdame to her son,"   189
Yea, let them say, to stick the heart of falsehood,   190
"As false as Cressid."

PANDARUS   Go to, a bargain made; seal it, seal it; I'll be
the witness. Here I hold your hand, here my cousin's. If
ever you prove false one to another, since I have taken
such pains to bring you together, let all pitiful goers-
between be called to the world's end after my name; call
them all Pandars. Let all constant men be Troiluses, all
false women Cressids, and all brokers-between Pandars!
Say "Amen."

TROILUS   Amen.   200

CRESSIDA   Amen.

PANDARUS   Amen. Whereupon I will show you a chamber, which bed, because it shall not speak of your pretty 203
encounters, press it to death. Away!

                      Exeunt [Troilus and Cressida].

And Cupid grant all tongue-tied maidens here
Bed, chamber, Pandar to provide this gear!   *Exit.* 206

                            *

❧ III.3 *[Flourish of trumpets.] Enter Ulysses, Diomedes,*
    Nestor, Agamemnon, [Menelaus, Ajax, and] Calchas.

CALCHAS
Now, princes, for the service I have done,
Th' advantage of the time prompts me aloud   2
To call for recompense. Appear it to mind   3
That through the sight I bear in things to love,   4
I have abandoned Troy, left my possession,
Incurred a traitor's name, exposed myself,

---

189 *Pard* leopard; *stepdame* stepmother   **190** *stick the heart of* pierce to the
center of   **203** *which bed* in which the bed; *because* so that   **206** *gear* appa-
ratus (of love)

    III.3 The Greek camp   **2** *advantage* opportunity   **3** *Appear it* let it appear
4 *sight* prophetic foresight

From certain and possessed conveniences,
8 To doubtful fortunes, sequest'ring from me all
That time, acquaintance, custom, and condition
10 Made tame and most familiar to my nature;
And here, to do you service, am become
As new into the world, strange, unacquainted.
13 I do beseech you, as in way of taste,
To give me now a little benefit
15 Out of those many registered in promise,
Which, you say, live to come in my behalf.

AGAMEMNON
What wouldst thou of us, Trojan? Make demand.

CALCHAS
You have a Trojan prisoner, called Antenor,
Yesterday took; Troy holds him very dear.
20 Oft have you – often have you thanks therefor –
21 Desired my Cressid in right great exchange,
Whom Troy hath still denied. But this Antenor
23 I know is such a wrest in their affairs
That their negotiations all must slack,
25 Wanting his manage; and they will almost
Give us a prince of blood, a son of Priam,
In change of him. Let him be sent, great princes,
And he shall buy my daughter; and her presence
29 Shall quite strike off all service I have done
30 In most accepted pain.

AGAMEMNON   Let Diomedes bear him,
And bring us Cressid hither. Calchas shall have
What he requests of us. Good Diomed,
33 Furnish you fairly for his interchange.
34 Withal bring word if Hector will tomorrow
Be answered in his challenge. Ajax is ready.

---

8 *sequest'ring from me* separating myself from   10 *tame* familiar   13 *as in way of taste* as a forestaste   15 *registered* recorded   21 *right great* very great   23 *wrest* tuning key for stringed instruments (i.e., key to harmony in Trojan affairs)   25 *Wanting his manage* lacking his management   29 *strike off* cancel   30 *accepted* willingly endured   33 *Furnish you fairly* equip yourself properly   34 *Withal* in addition

DIOMEDES

   This shall I undertake, and 'tis a burden

   Which I am proud to bear.   *Exit [with Calchas].*

   Achilles and Patroclus stand in their tent.

ULYSSES

   Achilles stands i' th' entrance of his tent.

   Please it our general to pass strangely by him,   39

   As if he were forgot; and, princes all,   40

   Lay negligent and loose regard upon him.

   I will come last. 'Tis like he'll question me   42

   Why such unplausive eyes are bent, why turned, on   43

     him.

   If so, I have derision med'cinable   44

   To use between your strangeness and his pride,   45

   Which his own will shall have desire to drink.   46

   It may do good. Pride hath no other glass   47

   To show itself but pride, for supple knees

   Feed arrogance and are the proud man's fees.

AGAMEMNON

   We'll execute your purpose, and put on   50

   A form of strangeness as we pass along.

   So do each lord, and either greet him not

   Or else disdainfully, which shall shake him more

   Than if not looked on. I will lead the way.

ACHILLES

   What comes the general to speak with me?

   You know my mind; I'll fight no more 'gainst Troy.

AGAMEMNON

   What says Achilles? Would he aught with us?

NESTOR

   Would you, my lord, aught with the general?

ACHILLES   No.

NESTOR   *[To Agamemnon]* Nothing, my lord.   60

---

39 *strangely* distantly   42 *like* likely   43 *unplausive* disapproving   44 *derision med'cinable* healing scorn   45 *use between* negotiate   46 *his own will . . . drink* i.e., his own inclination will make him want to understand   47–48 *Pride . . . pride* pride has no other mirror to reveal it to itself but pride (therefore let us be proud rather than deferential)

AGAMEMNON   The better.

ACHILLES   Good day, good day.

MENELAUS   How do you? How do you?

ACHILLES   What, does the cuckold scorn me?

AJAX   How now, Patroclus?

ACHILLES   Good morrow, Ajax.

AJAX   Ha?

ACHILLES   Good morrow.

AJAX   Ay, and good next day too.   *Exeunt.*

ACHILLES
70   What mean these fellows? Know they not Achilles?

PATROCLUS
They pass by strangely. They were used to bend,
To send their smiles before them to Achilles,
To come as humbly as they used to creep
To holy altars.

ACHILLES   What, am I poor of late?
75   'Tis certain, greatness, once fall'n out with fortune,
Must fall out with men too. What the declined is
He shall as soon read in the eyes of others
As feel in his own fall; for men, like butterflies,
79   Show not their mealy wings but to the summer,
80   And not a man, for being simply man,
Hath any honor, but honor for those honors
82   That are without him, as place, riches, and favor,
Prizes of accident as oft as merit;
84   Which when they fall, as being slippery standers,
The love that leaned on them as slippery too,
Doth one pluck down another, and together
Die in the fall. But 'tis not so with me;
Fortune and I are friends. I do enjoy
89   At ample point all that I did possess,
90   Save these men's looks; who do, methinks, find out

---

75 *fall'n . . . fortune* fallen out of fortune's favor   79 *mealy* powdered   82
without him external to him; *place* rank   84–86 *when . . . another* when they
fall, being on a precarious footing, as is the love that depends on their possession, they pull one another down   89 *At ample point* in full measure

Something not worth in me such rich beholding   91
As they have often given. Here is Ulysses;
I'll interrupt his reading.
How now, Ulysses.

ULYSSES   Now, great Thetis' son.

ACHILLES
What are you reading?

ULYSSES   A strange fellow here
Writes me that man, how dearly ever parted,   96
How much in having, or without or in,   97
Cannot make boast to have that which he hath,
Nor feels not what he owes but by reflection;   99
As when his virtues shining upon others   100
Heat them, and they retort that heat again   101
To the first giver.

ACHILLES   This is not strange, Ulysses.
The beauty that is borne here in the face
The bearer knows not, but commends itself
To others' eyes; nor doth the eye itself,
That most pure spirit of sense, behold itself,   106
Not going from itself; but eye to eye opposed   107
Salutes each other with each other's form;   108
For speculation turns not to itself   109
Till it hath traveled and is married there   110
Where it may see itself. This is not strange at all.

ULYSSES
I do not strain at the position –   112
It is familiar – but at the author's drift;   113
Who in his circumstance expressly proves   114

---

91 *rich beholding* attentive and admiring observation 96 *Writes me* writes;
dearly . . . parted richly endowed by nature (i.e., "parts" meaning personal
endowments) 97 *having* possession; *or without or in* outwardly or inwardly
99 *owes* owns 101 *retort* reflect back 106 *pure . . . sense* i.e., the purest and
most spiritual of the senses 107 *going from itself* moving outside of itself (its
fixed position) 108 *Salutes . . . form* i.e., the image one has of oneself is supplied by the perception of another 109 *speculation* vision 112 *strain at*
make an issue or difficulty of; *position* thesis, overall argument 113 *drift*
particular thrust 114 *circumstance* detailed exposition

That no man is the lord of anything –
116   Though in and of him there be much consisting –
117   Till he communicate his parts to others;
118   Nor doth he of himself know them for aught
119   Till he behold them formed in th' applause
120   Where they're extended; who, like an arch, reverb'rate
      The voice again, or, like a gate of steel
      Fronting the sun, receives and renders back
123   His figure and his heat. I was much rapt in this,
124   And apprehended here immediately
      Th' unknown Ajax. (Heavens, what a man is there!)
      A very horse, that has he knows not what.
      Nature, what things there are
128   Most abject in regard and dear in use!
129   What things again most dear in the esteem
130   And poor in worth! Now shall we see tomorrow,
      An act that very chance doth throw upon him.
      Ajax renowned? O heavens, what some men do,
133   While some men leave to do!
134   How some men creep in skittish Fortune's hall,
135   Whiles others play the idiots in her eyes!
136   How one man eats into another's pride,
      While pride is fasting in his wantonness!
      To see these Grecian lords! Why, even already
139   They clap the lubber Ajax on the shoulder,
140   As if his foot were on brave Hector's breast,
141   And great Troy shrinking.

---

116 *Though ... consisting* i.e., though he possesses and embodies many admirable qualities   117 *parts* personal endowments   118 *for aught* for what they are worth   119 *formed* given definition, realized   120 *extended* (1) brought out, (2) dispersed, (3) appreciated; *who* which; *reverb'rate* echo   123 *figure* image; *rapt* absorbed   124 *apprehended* recognized   128 *abject ... regard* viewed with disdain   129 *dear* valuable   133 *leave to do* leave undone   134 *creep in* insinuate themselves into; *skittish* capricious   135 *play the idiots* fail to capitalize on fortune's favor   136–37 *How ... wantonness* how one man encroaches on another's eminence while the pride of the other starves itself through self-satisfied negligence   139 *lubber* lout   141 *shrinking* i.e., shrinking before the final blow, following the defeat of Hector

ACHILLES
 I do believe it; for they passed by me
 As misers do by beggars, neither gave to me
 Good word nor look. What, are my deeds forgot?
ULYSSES
 Time hath, my lord, a wallet at his back,   145
 Wherein he puts alms for oblivion,   146
 A great-sized monster of ingratitudes.   147
 Those scraps are good deeds past, which are devoured
 As fast as they are made, forgot as soon
 As done. Perseverance, dear my lord,   150
 Keeps honor bright; to have done is to hang
 Quite out of fashion, like a rusty mail   152
 In monumental mock'ry. Take the instant way,   153
 For honor travels in a strait so narrow   154
 Where one but goes abreast. Keep, then, the path,   155
 For emulation hath a thousand sons   156
 That one by one pursue. If you give way,   157
 Or turn aside from the direct forthright,   158
 Like to an entered tide they all rush by   159
 And leave you hindmost;   160
 [Or, like a gallant horse fall'n in first rank,
 Lie there for pavement to the abject rear,   162
 O'errun and trampled on.] Then what they do in present,
 Though less than yours in past, must o'ertop yours.
 For time is like a fashionable host,
 That slightly shakes his parting guest by th' hand,   166
 And with his arms outstretched as he would fly,   167

---

145 *wallet* knapsack   146 *alms* charitable gifts (placatory offerings?); *oblivion*
(1) forgetfulness, (2) being blotted from memory   147 *monster . . . ingratitudes* i.e., forgetfulness is an enormous monster committing acts of ingrati-
tude (what should be gratefully remembered gets forgotten)   152 *mail* armor
153 *monumental mock'ry* mocking reminder or admonition; *instant* immedi-
ate   154 *strait* confined passage   155 *one but goes abreast* i.e., only one can
go through at a time   156 *emulation* (1) envious striving, (2) ambition
157 *That . . . pursue* who strive both after and against one another   158
forthright straight way   159 *entered tide* tide that has broken through or
flooded in   162 *abject rear* feeble, cowardly ones hanging back from the fray
166 *slightly* barely, negligently   167 *as* as if

168   Grasps in the comer. The welcome ever smiles,
       And farewell goes out sighing. Let not virtue seek
170   Remuneration for the thing it was. For beauty, wit,
       High birth, vigor of bone, desert in service,
       Love, friendship, charity, are subjects all
173   To envious and calumniating time.
174   One touch of nature makes the whole world kin,
175   That all with one consent praise new-born gawds,
       Though they are made and molded of things past,
177   And give to dust that is a little gilt
       More laud than gilt o'erdusted.
       The present eye praises the present object.
180   Then marvel not, thou great and complete man,
       That all the Greeks begin to worship Ajax,
       Since things in motion sooner catch the eye
183   Than what not stirs. The cry went once on thee,
       And still it might, and yet it may again,
       If thou wouldst not entomb thyself alive
186   And case thy reputation in thy tent,
       Whose glorious deeds, but in these fields of late,
188   Made emulous missions 'mongst the gods themselves
189   And drave great Mars to faction.

ACHILLES   Of this my privacy
190   I have strong reasons.

ULYSSES   But 'gainst your privacy
       The reasons are more potent and heroical.
       'Tis known, Achilles, that you are in love
193   With one of Priam's daughters.

ACHILLES   Ha? Known?

---

168 *comer* newcomer   173 *calumniating* slanderous   174 *One touch . . . kin*
one natural weakness (here, the praise of the new) unites humanity   175
new-born gawds novel fripperies or playthings   177–78 *give . . . o'erdusted*
give gilded dirt more praise than dusty gold   183 *cry . . . thee* you were once
acclaimed   186 *case* enclose   188 *emulous . . . themselves* i.e., the envious
gods joined in the fighting   189 *drave* drove; *faction* take sides   193 *one of
Priam's daughters* i.e., Polyxena

ULYSSES
   Is that a wonder?
   The providence that's in a watchful state   196
   Knows almost every grain of Pluto's gold,   197
   Finds bottom in th' uncomprehensive deeps,   198
   Keeps place with thought, and almost, like the gods,   199
   Does thoughts unveil in their dumb cradles.   *200*
   There is a mystery – with whom relation   201
   Durst never meddle – in the soul of state,
   Which hath an operation more divine
   Than breath or pen can give expressure to.   204
   All the commerce that you have had with Troy   205
   As perfectly is ours as yours, my lord;   206
   And better would it fit Achilles much
   To throw down Hector than Polyxena.   208
   But it must grieve young Pyrrhus now at home,   209
   When fame shall in our islands sound her trump,   210
   And all the Greekish girls shall tripping sing,
   "Great Hector's sister did Achilles win,
   But our great Ajax bravely beat down him."
   Farewell, my lord. I as your lover speak;   214
   The fool slides o'er the ice that you should break.   215
                         [Exit.]

PATROCLUS
   To this effect, Achilles, have I moved you.   216
   A woman impudent and mannish grown
   Is not more loathed than an effeminate man

---

196 *providence* precautionary oversight   **197** *Pluto's* (belonging to the god of
the underworld, here conflated with Plutus, god of riches)   **198** *uncomprehensive* unfathomable   **199** *Keeps . . . thought* i.e., knows what is thought
even as it is being thought   **201** *mystery* (1) secret, (2) craft; *relation*
open discussion   **204** *expressure* expression   **205** *commerce* transactions
206 *is ours as yours* is as well known to us as it is to you   **208** *throw down*
conquer (militarily rather than sexually, as in the case of Polyxena)   **209**
Pyrrhus son of Achilles   **210** *trump* trumpet   **214** *lover* friend   **215** *The
fool . . . break* i.e., Ajax (the *fool*) can get away with things you cannot   **216**
moved urged

In time of action. I stand condemned for this.
220 They think my little stomach to the war
And your great love to me restrains you thus.
Sweet, rouse yourself, and the weak wanton Cupid
223 Shall from your neck unloose his amorous fold
And, like a dewdrop from the lion's mane,
Be shook to air.

ACHILLES   Shall Ajax fight with Hector?

PATROCLUS
Ay, and perhaps receive much honor by him.

ACHILLES
I see my reputation is at stake;
228 My fame is shrewdly gored.

PATROCLUS   O, then, beware!
Those wounds heal ill that men do give themselves.
230 Omission to do what is necessary
231 Seals a commission to a blank of danger;
232 And danger, like an ague, subtly taints
Even then when we sit idly in the sun.

ACHILLES
Go call Thersites hither, sweet Patroclus.
I'll send the fool to Ajax and desire him
T' invite the Trojan lords after the combat
237 To see us here unarmed. I have a woman's longing,
An appetite that I am sick withal,
239 To see great Hector in his weeds of peace,
240 To talk with him and to behold his visage,
Even to my full of view. A labor saved!

      Enter Thersites.

242 THERSITES   A wonder!

ACHILLES   What?

---

223 *fold* embrace   **228** *shrewdly gored* hurtfully pierced   **231** *Seals . . . danger* signs a blank draft for danger (i.e., lays one open to unknown dangers) **232** *an ague* a fever; *taints* infects   **237** *a woman's longing* i.e., a craving like a pregnant woman's, but possibly implying sexual desire as well   **239** *weeds* garments   **242** *wonder* miracle

THERSITES　Ajax goes up and down the field, asking for　244
himself.

ACHILLES　How so?

THERSITES　He must fight singly tomorrow with Hector,
and is so prophetically proud of an heroical cudgeling
that he raves in saying nothing.　249

ACHILLES　How can that be?　250

THERSITES　Why, a stalks up and down like a peacock, a
stride and a stand; ruminates like an hostess that hath　252
no arithmetic but her brain to set down her reckoning;
bites his lip with a politic regard, as who should say,　254
"There were wit in this head an 'twould out" – and so　255
there is, but it lies as coldly in him as fire in a flint,
which will not show without knocking. The man's undone for ever, for if Hector break not his neck i' th'
combat, he'll break't himself in vainglory. He knows
not me. I said, "Good morrow, Ajax"; and he replies,　260
"Thanks, Agamemnon." What think you of this man
that takes me for the general? He's grown a very land
fish, languageless, a monster. A plague of opinion! A　263
man may wear it on both sides like a leather jerkin.

ACHILLES　Thou must be my ambassador to him, Thersites.

THERSITES　Who, I? Why, he'll answer nobody. He pro-　267
fesses not answering; speaking is for beggars. He wears　268
his tongue in's arms. I will put on his presence. Let Pa-　269
troclus make demands to me. You shall see the pageant　270
of Ajax.

244–45 *asking for himself* (possible pun on his name: "a jakes," meaning a privy – a common, antiheroic pun in Shakespeare's time)　249 *raves . . . nothing* babbles senselessly　252–53 *hostess . . . brain* tavern hostess capable of adding up the bill only through slow mental arithmetic　254 *politic regard* wise look　255 *an* if　263 *of* on　263–64 *A man . . . jerkin* i.e., opinion is reversible, like a leather jacket (the opinion that Ajax is a boastful fool can be turned inside out to make him heroic)　267–68 *professes . . . answering* (1) does not undertake to answer, (2) makes a principle of not answering　268–69 *wears . . . arms* i.e., his weapons speak for him　269 *presence* demeanor　270 *make demands* ask questions; *pageant* stage play

ACHILLES To him, Patroclus. Tell him I humbly desire
the valiant Ajax to invite the most valorous Hector to
come unarmed to my tent, and to procure safe-conduct
for his person of the magnanimous and most illustrious
six-or-seven-times-honored captain-general of the Grecian army, Agamemnon, et cetera. Do this.

PATROCLUS *[To Thersites]* Jove bless great Ajax!

279 THERSITES Hum!

280 PATROCLUS I come from the worthy Achilles –

THERSITES Ha!

PATROCLUS Who most humbly desires you to invite
Hector to his tent –

THERSITES Hum!

PATROCLUS And to procure safe-conduct from Agamemnon.

THERSITES Agamemnon?

PATROCLUS Ay, my lord.

THERSITES Ha!

290 PATROCLUS What say you to't?

THERSITES God be wi' you, with all my heart.

PATROCLUS Your answer, sir.

THERSITES If tomorrow be a fair day, by eleven of the
clock it will go one way or other. Howsoever, he shall
pay for me ere he has me.

PATROCLUS Your answer, sir.

THERSITES Fare ye well, with all my heart. *[Performance
ends.]*

298 ACHILLES Why, but he is not in this tune, is he?

THERSITES No, but out of tune thus. What music will be

300 in him when Hector has knocked out his brains, I

301 know not; but I am sure none, unless the fiddler Apollo

302 get his sinews to make catlings on.

ACHILLES Come, thou shalt bear a letter to him straight.

---

279 *Hum* (surly exclamation) **298** *tune* mode, frame of mind **301** *fiddler*
(as patron deity of music, *Apollo* was often pictured with a lyre) **302** *catlings*
strings of catgut

THERSITES   Let me bear another to his horse, for that's
the more capable creature.

ACHILLES
My mind is troubled, like a fountain stirred,
And I myself see not the bottom of it.
                              [Exeunt Achilles and Patroclus.]

THERSITES   Would the fountain of your mind were clear
again, that I might water an ass at it! I had rather be a   309
tick in a sheep than such a valiant ignorance.   *[Exit.]*   310

                              *

❧ **IV.1** *Enter, at one door, Aeneas [with a torchbearer];
at another, Paris, Deiphobus, Antenor, Diomed the
Grecian, [and others,] with torches.*

PARIS
See, ho! Who is that there?

DEIPHOBUS   It is the Lord Aeneas.

AENEAS
Is the prince there in person?
Had I so good occasion to lie long   3
As you, Prince Paris, nothing but heavenly business
Should rob my bedmate of my company.

DIOMEDES
That's my mind too. Good morrow, Lord Aeneas.

PARIS
A valiant Greek, Aeneas; take his hand.
Witness the process of your speech, wherein   8
You told how Diomed, a whole week by days,   9
Did haunt you in the field.   10

AENEAS   Health to you, valiant sir,
During all question of the gentle truce;   11

---

309 *water* bring to drink
   IV.1 Within the city of Troy   **3** *occasion* cause   **8** *Witness . . . speech* i.e.,
let the tenor of your statements again bear witness   **9** *by days* day after day
11 *question . . . truce* discussions we will have during this time of truce

> But when I meet you armed, as black defiance
> As heart can think or courage execute.

DIOMEDES
> The one and other Diomed embraces.
15   Our bloods are now in calm, and, so long, health;
16   But when contention and occasion meet,
> By Jove, I'll play the hunter for thy life
18   With all my force, pursuit, and policy.

AENEAS
> And thou shalt hunt a lion that will fly
20   With his face backward. In humane gentleness,
21   Welcome to Troy. Now, by Anchises' life,
22   Welcome indeed! By Venus' hand I swear,
23   No man alive can love in such a sort
> The thing he means to kill more excellently.

DIOMEDES
25   We sympathize. Jove, let Aeneas live,
> If to my sword his fate be not the glory,
27   A thousand complete courses of the sun!
28   But, in mine emulous honor, let him die
> With every joint a wound, and that tomorrow!

AENEAS
30   We know each other well.

DIOMEDES
> We do, and long to know each other worse.

PARIS
32   This is the most despiteful gentle greeting,
> The noblest hateful love, that e'er I heard of.
> What business, lord, so early?

AENEAS
> I was sent for to the king; but why, I know not.

PARIS
36   His purpose meets you. 'Twas to bring this Greek

---

15 *so long* for as long as the truce lasts   16 *occasion* opportunity   18 *policy* cunning   21 *Anchises* (Aeneas's father)   22 *Venus* (Aeneas's mother)   23 *in such a sort* to such a degree   25 *sympathize* feel the same way, concur   27 *courses of the sun* years   28 *emulous* aspiring   32 *despiteful* malign   36 *meets you* i.e., in my person, as I shall now deliver it

To Calchas' house, and there to render him,   37
For the enfreed Antenor, the fair Cressid.
Let's have your company, or, if you please,
Haste there before us. *[Aside to Aeneas]* I constantly do 40
   think –
Or rather call my thought a certain knowledge –
My brother Troilus lodges there tonight.
Rouse him and give him note of our approach,   43
With the whole quality wherefore. I fear   44
We shall be much unwelcome.
AENEAS   *[Aside to Paris]*   That I assure you.
Troilus had rather Troy were borne to Greece
Than Cressid borne from Troy.
PARIS   *[Aside to Aeneas]*   There is no help.
The bitter disposition of the time   48
Will have it so. On, lord; we'll follow you.
AENEAS
Good morrow, all.   *[Exit Aeneas.]* 50
PARIS
And tell me, noble Diomed, faith, tell me true,
Even in the soul of sound good-fellowship,
Who, in your thoughts, deserves fair Helen best,
Myself or Menelaus?
DIOMEDES   Both alike.
He merits well to have her that doth seek her,
Not making any scruple of her soilure,   56
With such a hell of pain and world of charge;   57
And you as well to keep her that defend her,
Not palating the taste of her dishonor,   59
With such a costly loss of wealth and friends.   60
He, like a puling cuckold, would drink up   61
The lees and dregs of a flat, tamèd piece;   62

---

37 *render* give in exchange   40 *constantly* firmly   43 *note* notice   44 *quality*
cause, occasion   48 *disposition* nature, condition   56 *soilure* defilement   57
charge cost   59 *Not palating* not tasting, insensible of   61 *puling* whining
62 *lees* sediment; *flat, tamèd piece* cask left open so long that the wine has
gone flat

You, like a lecher, out of whorish loins
Are pleased to breed out your inheritors.
65   Both merits poised, each weighs nor less nor more;
66   But he as he, the heavier for a whore.

PARIS
You are too bitter to your countrywoman.

DIOMEDES
She's bitter to her country. Hear me, Paris:
For every false drop in her bawdy veins
70   A Grecian's life hath sunk. For every scruple
71   Of her contaminated carrion weight
A Trojan hath been slain. Since she could speak,
She hath not given so many good words breath
As for her Greeks and Trojans suffered death.

PARIS
75   Fair Diomed, you do as chapmen do,
Dispraise the thing that you desire to buy;
But we in silence hold this virtue well,
We'll not commend what we intend to sell.
Here lies our way.   *Exeunt.*

*

∾ **IV.2** *Enter Troilus and Cressida.*

TROILUS
Dear, trouble not yourself. The morn is cold.

CRESSIDA
Then, sweet my lord, I'll call mine uncle down.
He shall unbolt the gates.

TROILUS   Trouble him not.
4   To bed, to bed! Sleep kill those pretty eyes,
5   And give as soft attachment to thy senses
As infants' empty of all thought!

---

65 *poised* balanced 66 *he as he* i.e., both alike 70 *scruple* infinitesimal
amount 71 *carrion* rotten 75 *chapmen* merchants
   IV.2 Calchas's house 4 *kill* close up 5 *attachment* arrest

CRESSIDA   Good morrow, then.

TROILUS

I prithee now, to bed.

CRESSIDA   Are you aweary of me?

TROILUS

O Cressida, but that the busy day,

Waked by the lark, hath roused the ribald crows,   9

And dreaming night will hide our joys no longer,   10

I would not from thee.

CRESSIDA   Night hath been too brief.

TROILUS

Beshrew the witch! With venomous wights she stays   12

As tediously as hell, but flies the grasps of love

With wings more momentary-swift than thought.

You will catch cold and curse me.

CRESSIDA

Prithee, tarry; you men will never tarry.

O foolish Cressid! I might have still held off,

And then you would have tarried. Hark, there's one up.

PANDARUS   *[Within]* What's all the doors open here?

TROILUS   It is your uncle.   20

CRESSIDA   A pestilence on him! Now will he be mocking.   21

I shall have such a life.

          Enter Pandarus.

PANDARUS   How now, how now, how go maidenheads?

Here, you maid, where's my cousin Cressid?

CRESSIDA

Go hang yourself, you naughty mocking uncle.

You bring me to do – and then you flout me too.   26

PANDARUS   To do what? To do what? Let her say what.

What have I brought you to do?

CRESSIDA

Come, come; beshrew your heart! You'll ne'er be good,

---

9 *ribald* obnoxiously raucous   12 *Beshrew the witch* i.e., curses upon night;
venomous wights malignant, evil people; *stays* tarries   21 *pestilence* plague
26 *flout* tease

30   Nor suffer others.
31 PANDARUS   Ha, ha! Alas, poor wretch! A poor *capocchia!*
32   Hast not slept tonight? Would he not – ah, naughty
33   man – let it sleep! A bugbear take him!
   CRESSIDA
34   Did not I tell you? Would he were knocked i' th' head!
      One knocks.
      Who's that at door? Good uncle, go and see.
      My lord, come you again into my chamber.
      You smile and mock me, as if I meant naughtily.
   TROILUS   Ha, ha!
   CRESSIDA
      Come, you are deceived, I think of no such thing.
      Knock.
40   How earnestly they knock! Pray you, come in.
      I would not for half Troy have you seen here.
                        Exeunt [Troilus and Cressida].
   PANDARUS   Who's there? What's the matter? Will you
      beat down the door? How now, what's the matter?
      [Enter Aeneās.]
   AENEAS
      Good morrow, lord, good morrow.
   PANDARUS   Who's there? My Lord Aeneas! By my troth, I
      knew you not. What news with you so early?
   AENEAS
      Is not Prince Troilus here?
   PANDARUS   Here? What should he do here?
   AENEAS
49   Come, he is here, my lord. Do not deny him.
50   It doth import him much to speak with me.

PANDARUS   Is he here, say you? It's more than I know, I'll
be sworn. For my own part I came in late. What should
he do here?

AENEAS   Ho, nay then! Come, come, you'll do him
wrong ere you are ware. You'll be so true to him, to be   55
false to him. Do not you know of him, but yet go fetch   56
him hither. Go.

    [Enter Troilus.]

TROILUS   How now, what's the matter?

AENEAS
My lord, I scarce have leisure to salute you,
My matter is so rash. There is at hand   60
Paris your brother, and Deiphobus,
The Grecian Diomed, and our Antenor
Delivered to us; and for him forthwith,
Ere the first sacrifice, within this hour,
We must give up to Diomedes' hand
The Lady Cressida.   66

TROILUS   Is it concluded so?

AENEAS
By Priam and the general state of Troy.   67
They are at hand and ready to effect it.

TROILUS
How my achievements mock me!
I will go meet them. And, my Lord Aeneas,   70
We met by chance; you did not find me here.

AENEAS
Good, good, my lord; the secrets of nature   72
Have not more gift in taciturnity.

                Exeunt [Troilus and Aeneas].

PANDARUS   Is't possible? No sooner got but lost? The
devil take Antenor! The young prince will go mad. A
plague upon Antenor! I would they had broke 's neck!

---

55 *ware* aware   56–57 *Do not you . . . hither* i.e., do not carry on your pre-
tense that you don't know his whereabouts, but bring him here   60 *rash*
urgent; *at hand* nearby   66 *concluded* resolved, agreed   67 *general state*
governing council   72–73 *the secrets . . . taciturnity* (nature was believed to
be reluctant to yield up its secrets)

Enter Cressida.

CRESSIDA
How now? What's the matter? Who was here?

PANDARUS   Ah, ah!

CRESSIDA
Why sigh you so profoundly? Where's my lord?

80   Gone? Tell me, sweet uncle, what's the matter?

PANDARUS   Would I were as deep under the earth as I am
above!

CRESSIDA   O the gods! What's the matter?

PANDARUS   Pray thee, get thee in. Would thou hadst
ne'er been born! I knew thou wouldst be his death. O
poor gentleman! A plague upon Antenor!

CRESSIDA   Good uncle, I beseech you, on my knees I beseech you, what's the matter?

PANDARUS   Thou must be gone, wench, thou must be
90   gone. Thou art changed for Antenor. Thou must to thy
father and be gone from Troilus. 'Twill be his death;
92   'twill be his bane; he cannot bear it.

CRESSIDA
O you immortal gods! I will not go.

PANDARUS   Thou must.

CRESSIDA
I will not, uncle. I have forgot my father.
96   I know no touch of consanguinity –
No kin, no love, no blood, no soul so near me
As the sweet Troilus. O you gods divine,
Make Cressid's name the very crown of falsehood
100   If ever she leave Troilus! Time, force, and death,
Do to this body what extremes you can;
102   But the strong base and building of my love
Is as the very center of the earth,
Drawing all things to it. I'll go in and weep.

PANDARUS   Do, do.

---

90 *changed* exchanged   **92** *bane* mortal injury or poison   **96** *consanguinity*
blood relationship   **102** *base* foundation

CRESSIDA
　Tear my bright hair, and scratch my praisèd cheeks,
　Crack my clear voice with sobs, and break my heart
　With sounding Troilus. I will not go from Troy.
　　　　　　　　　　　　　　　　　[Exeunt.]

∗

∾ **IV.3**　*Enter Paris, Troilus, Aeneas, Deiphobus,*
　　Antenor, Diomedes.

PARIS
　It is great morning, and the hour prefixed　　　　　1
　For her delivery to this valiant Greek
　Comes fast upon. Good my brother Troilus,
　Tell you the lady what she is to do,
　And haste her to the purpose.
TROILUS　　　　　　　　　　　Walk into her house.
　I'll bring her to the Grecian presently;　　　　　6
　And to his hand when I deliver her,
　Think it an altar, and thy brother Troilus
　A priest there off'ring to it his own heart.
PARIS
　I know what 'tis to love;　　　　　　　　　　　*10*
　And would, as I shall pity, I could help!　　　　*11*
　Please you walk in, my lords.　　　　　*Exeunt.*

∗

∾ **IV.4**　*Enter Pandarus and Cressida.*

PANDARUS　Be moderate, be moderate.
CRESSIDA
　Why tell you me of moderation?

IV.3 Calchas's house　**1** *great morning* broad daylight; *prefixed* prearranged
6 *presently* immediately　**11** *And would . . . help* i.e., I wish I could help you
as much as I shall pity you
　IV.4 Calchas's house

3   The grief is fine, full, perfect, that I taste,

4   And violenteth in a sense as strong
      As that which causeth it. How can I moderate it?

6   If I could temporize with my affections,

7   Or brew it to a weak and colder palate,

8   The like allayment could I give my grief.

9   My love admits no qualifying dross;

10   No more my grief, in such a precious loss.
      Enter Troilus.

PANDARUS   Here, here, here he comes. Ah, sweet ducks!

CRESSIDA   *[Embracing him]* O Troilus! Troilus!

13 PANDARUS   What a pair of spectacles is here! Let me em-
      brace too. "O heart," as the goodly saying is –
           "O heart, heavy heart,
           Why sigh'st thou without breaking?"
      where he answers again,
            "Because thou canst not ease thy smart
            By friendship nor by speaking."

20 There was never a truer rhyme. Let us cast away noth-
      ing, for we may live to have need of such a verse. We see
      it, we see it. How now, lambs?

TROILUS

23 Cressid, I love thee in so strained a purity,

24 That the blest gods, as angry with my fancy –
      More bright in zeal than the devotion which
      Cold lips blow to their deities – take thee from me.

CRESSIDA   Have the gods envy?

PANDARUS   Ay, ay, ay, ay; 'tis too plain a case.

CRESSIDA
      And is it true that I must go from Troy?

TROILUS

30 A hateful truth.

---

3 *fine* pure; *perfect* unsurpassable, complete 4 *violenteth . . . strong* rages
with the same force 6 *temporize* manipulate, bargain with 7 *palate* taste
8 *allayment* dilution, mitigation 9 *qualifying dross* contaminating admix-
ture 10 *precious loss* loss of what is precious 13 *What a pair . . . is here*
what a spectacle the two of you make 23 *strained* filtered, purified 24
fancy love

CRESSIDA   What, and from Troilus too?
TROILUS
  From Troy and Troilus.
CRESSIDA   Is't possible?
TROILUS
  And suddenly, where injury of chance   32
  Puts back leave-taking, justles roughly by   33
  All time of pause, rudely beguiles our lips
  Of all rejoindure, forcibly prevents   35
  Our locked embrasures, strangles our dear vows   36
  Even in the birth of our own laboring breath.
  We two, that with so many thousand sighs
  Did buy each other, must poorly sell ourselves
  With the rude brevity and discharge of one.   40
  Injurious time now with a robber's haste
  Crams his rich thiev'ry up, he knows not how.
  As many farewells as be stars in heaven,
  With distinct breath and consigned kisses to them,   44
  He fumbles up into a loose adieu,   45
  And scants us with a single famished kiss,   46
  Distasted with the salt of broken tears.   47
AENEAS   (Within) My lord, is the lady ready?
TROILUS
  Hark! You are called. Some say the Genius   49
  Cries so to him that instantly must die.   50
  Bid them have patience. She shall come anon.
PANDARUS   Where are my tears? Rain, to lay this wind,   52
  or my heart will be blown up by the root!   [Exit.]
CRESSIDA
  I must, then, to the Grecians?
TROILUS   No remedy.

---

32 *injury of chance* injurious chance   33 *Puts back* forestalls, prohibits; *justles*
jostles   35 *rejoindure* (1) reunion, (2) retort   36 *embrasures* embraces   40
one i.e., sigh   44 *With . . . them* i.e., farewells distinctly uttered and dis-
patched to heaven with kisses   45 *fumbles up* clumsily bundles together;
loose lax, unceremonious   46 *scants us* denies us adequate provision   47
Distasted made unpalatable; *broken* interrupted, sporadically renewed   49
Genius attendant personal spirit   52 *lay* quieten

CRESSIDA
    A woeful Cressid 'mongst the merry Greeks!
    When shall we see again?
TROILUS
    Hear me, love. Be thou but true of heart –
CRESSIDA
58   I true! How now! What wicked deem is this?
TROILUS
59   Nay, we must use expostulation kindly,
60   For it is parting from us.
61   I speak not "Be thou true" as fearing thee,
62   For I will throw my glove to Death himself
63   That there's no maculation in thy heart;
64   But "Be thou true," say I, to fashion in
    My sequent protestation: be thou true,
    And I will see thee.
CRESSIDA
    O, you shall be exposed, my lord, to dangers
    As infinite as imminent. But I'll be true.
TROILUS
69   And I'll grow friend with danger. Wear this sleeve.
CRESSIDA
70   And you this glove. When shall I see you?
TROILUS
71   I will corrupt the Grecian sentinels,
    To give thee nightly visitation.
    But yet, be true.
CRESSIDA   O heavens! "Be true" again!
TROILUS
    Hear why I speak it, love.
75   The Grecian youths are full of quality;

---

58 *deem* supposition   59–60 *Nay . . . us* i.e., let's tax each other gently, since
the chance to do even that is passing   61 *fearing* distrusting   62 *throw my
glove to* challenge   63 *maculation* stain, taint   64–65 *to fashion in . . . protes-
tation* i.e., to link it to what follows (*I will see thee*)   69 *sleeve* (detachable
sleeve given as a love token)   71 *corrupt* bribe   75 *quality* good qualities,
lively appeal

[They're loving, well composed, with gift of nature,]   76
And swelling o'er with arts and exercise.   77
How novelty may move, and parts with person,   78
Alas! a kind of godly jealousy –
Which, I beseech you, call a virtuous sin –   80
Makes me afeard.

CRESSIDA   O heavens, you love me not!

TROILUS
Die I a villain, then!
In this I do not call your faith in question
So mainly as my merit. I cannot sing,   84
Nor heel the high lavolt, nor sweeten talk,   85
Nor play at subtle games – fair virtues all,   86
To which the Grecians are most prompt and pregnant.   87
But I can tell that in each grace of these
There lurks a still and dumb-discoursive devil   89
That tempts most cunningly. But be not tempted.   90

CRESSIDA   Do you think I will?

TROILUS   No.
But something may be done that we will not;   93
And sometimes we are devils to ourselves
When we will tempt the frailty of our powers,
Presuming on their changeful potency.   96

AENEAS   *Within*
Nay, good my lord!   97

TROILUS   Come, kiss, and let us part.

PARIS   *Within*
Brother Troilus!

TROILUS   Good brother, come you hither;

---

76 *They're loving . . . gift of nature* i.e., they are well framed for courtship by
their natural endowments   77 *swelling o'er . . . arts and exercise* abundantly
endowed with well-honed skills   78 *parts with person* accomplishments coupled with good looks   84 *mainly* strongly   85 *high lavolt* vigorous, skipping
dance; *sweeten talk* make my speech mellifluous   86 *subtle* requiring skill or
artfulness   87 *prompt and pregnant* ready and able   89 *still* quiet; *dumb-
discoursive* silently speaking   93 *will not* do not wish or mean   96 *changeful
potency* variable strength   97 *Nay, good my lord* i.e., please finish now

And bring Aeneas and the Grecian with you.

CRESSIDA

100   My lord, will you be true?

TROILUS

Who, I? Alas, it is my vice, my fault.

102   Whiles others fish with craft for great opinion,
103   I with great truth catch mere simplicity;
104   Whilst some with cunning gild their copper crowns,
105   With truth and plainness I do wear mine bare.
106   Fear not my truth. The moral of my wit
Is "plain and true"; there's all the reach of it.
*[Enter Aeneas, Paris, Antenor, Deiphobus, and
Diomedes.]*
Welcome, Sir Diomed. Here is the lady
Which for Antenor we deliver you.
110   At the port, lord, I'll give her to thy hand,
111   And by the way possess thee what she is.
112   Entreat her fair, and, by my soul, fair Greek,
If e'er thou stand at mercy of my sword,
Name Cressid, and thy life shall be as safe
As Priam is in Ilion.

DIOMEDES   Fair Lady Cressid,
So please you, save the thanks this prince expects.
The luster in your eye, heaven in your cheek,
Pleads your fair usage; and to Diomed
119   You shall be mistress, and command him wholly.

TROILUS

120   Grecian, thou dost not use me courteously,
121   To shame the seal of my petition to thee
In praising her. I tell thee, lord of Greece,
She is as far high-soaring o'er thy praises

---

102 *fish . . . great opinion* craftily solicit high esteem   103 *catch mere simplicity* i.e., come across as (1) simply honest, (2) simple-witted   104 *crowns* (1)
coins, (2) headgear   105 *mine* i.e., my head   106 *moral of my wit* maxim
that crystallizes my thought   110 *port* gate   111 *possess* inform   112 *Entreat* treat   119 *mistress* object of chaste, courtly devotion (but Diomedes
is already implying more)   121 *shame . . . petition* i.e., insultingly violate the
solemn undertaking I made in requesting that you treat her well

As thou unworthy to be called her servant.
I charge thee use her well, even for my charge;   125
For, by the dreadful Pluto, if thou dost not,
Though the great bulk Achilles be thy guard,   127
I'll cut thy throat.
DIOMEDES   O, be not moved, Prince Troilus.
Let me be privileged by my place and message
To be a speaker free. When I am hence,   130
I'll answer to my lust; and know you, lord,   131
I'll nothing do on charge. To her own worth   132
She shall be prized; but that you say "Be't so,"
I'll speak it in my spirit and honor, "No."
TROILUS
Come, to the port. I'll tell thee, Diomed,
This brave shall oft make thee to hide thy head.   136
Lady, give me your hand, and, as we walk,
To our own selves bend we our needful talk.
            [Exeunt Troilus, Cressida, and Diomedes.]
    Sound trumpet.
PARIS
Hark! Hector's trumpet.   139
AENEAS   How have we spent this morn-
    ing!
The prince must think me tardy and remiss,   140
That swore to ride before him to the field.
PARIS
'Tis Troilus' fault. Come, come, to field with him.
[DEIPHOBUS
Let us make ready straight.
AENEAS
Yea, with a bridegroom's fresh alacrity,
Let us address to tend on Hector's heels.   145
The glory of our Troy doth this day lie
On his fair worth and single chivalry.]   *Exeunt.*   147

---

125 *even for my charge* simply because I have charged you   127 *bulk* hulk
131 *answer to my lust* do as I please   132 *on charge* at someone else's bidding
136 *brave* boast   139 *spent* wasted   145 *address* prepare   147 *single chivalry*
prowess in individual combat

*

∾ **IV.5** *Enter Ajax, armed; Achilles, Patroclus,*
Agamemnon, Menelaus, Ulysses, Nestor, Calchas, etc.
[and Trumpeter].

AGAMEMNON

1   Here art thou in appointment fresh and fair,
2   Anticipating time. With starting courage,
     Give with thy trumpet a loud note to Troy,
4   Thou dreadful Ajax, that the appallèd air
     May pierce the head of the great combatant
6   And hale him hither.

AJAX   Thou, trumpet, there's my purse.
     Now crack thy lungs and split thy brazen pipe.
8   Blow, villain, till thy spherèd bias cheek
9   Outswell the colic of puffed Aquilon.
10   Come, stretch thy chest, and let thy eyes spout blood;
     Thou blowest for Hector.
     [Trumpet sounds.]

ULYSSES

12   No trumpet answers.

ACHILLES   'Tis but early days.

AGAMEMNON

13   Is not yond Diomed with Calchas' daughter?

ULYSSES

14   'Tis he, I ken the manner of his gait;
     He rises on the toe. That spirit of his
     In aspiration lifts him from the earth.
     [Enter Diomedes, with Cressida.]

AGAMEMNON

     Is this the Lady Cressid?

IV.5 The Greek camp **1** *appointment* equipment **2** *starting* barely reined
in **4** *dreadful* fearsome; *appallèd* terrified, violently disturbed **6** *hale* haul;
trumpet trumpeter **8** *villain* wretch; *bias* puffed out **9** *colic . . . Aquilon*
i.e., the personified north wind, distended by colic **12** *early days* early in the
day **13** *Calchas' daughter* Cressida **14** *ken* know

DIOMEDES   Even she.

AGAMEMNON

Most dearly welcome to the Greeks, sweet lady. *[Kisses her.]*

NESTOR

Our general doth salute you with a kiss.

ULYSSES

Yet is the kindness but particular.   20

'Twere better she were kissed in general.   21

NESTOR

And very courtly counsel. I'll begin.

So much for Nestor. *[Kisses her.]*

ACHILLES

I'll take that winter from your lips, fair lady.   24

Achilles bids you welcome. *[Kisses her.]*

MENELAUS

I had good argument for kissing once.   26

PATROCLUS

But that's no argument for kissing now;

For thus popped Paris in his hardiment,   28

And parted thus you and your argument. *[Kisses her.]*   29

ULYSSES

O, deadly gall, and theme of all our scorns,   30

For which we lose our heads to gild his horns!   31

PATROCLUS

The first was Menelaus' kiss; this, mine:

Patroclus kisses you. *[Kisses her again.]*   33

MENELAUS   O, this is trim.

PATROCLUS

Paris and I kiss evermore for him.   34

---

20 *particular* individual   21 *in general* i.e., (1) not just by the general but by everyone, (2) as a rule   24 *take that winter* i.e., aged Nestor's chilly kiss   26 *argument* reason, motive   28 *popped* intervened; *hardiment* boldness   29 *argument* i.e., Helen   30 *gall* annoyance, injury; *theme . . . scorns* topic of our mockery and source of our humiliation   31 *lose our heads* (1) are killed in battle, (2) act irrationally; *gild his horns* i.e., to make Menelaus, the cuckold, look good   33 *trim* nicely done (ironic)   34 *Paris . . . him* i.e., Paris and I both kiss in Menelaus's place

MENELAUS
> I'll have my kiss, sir. Lady, by your leave.

CRESSIDA
36   In kissing, do you render or receive?

PATROCLUS
37   Both take and give.

CRESSIDA   I'll make my match to live,
> The kiss you take is better than you give;
> Therefore no kiss.

MENELAUS
40   I'll give you boot; I'll give you three for one.

CRESSIDA
41   You are an odd man; give even, or give none.

MENELAUS
> An odd man, lady? Every man is odd.

CRESSIDA
> No, Paris is not, for you know 'tis true
> That you are odd and he is even with you.

MENELAUS
45   You fillip me o' th' head.

CRESSIDA   No, I'll be sworn.

ULYSSES
46   It were no match, your nail against his horn.
> May I, sweet lady, beg a kiss of you?

CRESSIDA
> You may.

ULYSSES   I do desire it.

CRESSIDA   Why, beg then.

ULYSSES
> Why, then, for Venus' sake, give me a kiss,
50   When Helen is a maid again, and his –

CRESSIDA
> I am your debtor; claim it when 'tis due.

---

36 *render* give 37 *make . . . live* I'll bet my life 40 *boot* odds 41 *odd* strange, singular 45 *fillip* tap 46 *nail . . . horn* i.e., your fingernail would make no impression on his horn 50 *When . . . his* when Helen is a virgin again, and back in Menelaus's possession (i.e., never)

ULYSSES
  Never's my day, and then a kiss of you.
DIOMEDES
  Lady, a word. I'll bring you to your father.
                    [Exeunt Diomedes and Cressida.]
NESTOR
  A woman of quick sense.   54
ULYSSES   Fie, fie upon her!
  There's language in her eye, her cheek, her lip;
  Nay, her foot speaks. Her wanton spirits look out
  At every joint and motive of her body.   57
  O, these encounterers, so glib of tongue,
  That give a coasting welcome ere it comes,   59
  And wide unclasp the tables of their thoughts   60
  To every ticklish reader. Set them down   61
  For sluttish spoils of opportunity
  And daughters of the game.
      Flourish. Enter all of Troy [Hector, Paris, Aeneas,
      Helenus, Troilus, and Attendants].
ALL
  The Trojans' trumpet.
AGAMEMNON   Yonder comes the troop.
AENEAS
  Hail, all you state of Greece. What shall be done   65
  To him that victory commands? Or do you purpose   66
  A victor shall be known? Will you the knights   67
  Shall to the edge of all extremity   68
  Pursue each other, or shall they be divided   69
  By any voice or order of the field?   70
  Hector bade ask.

---

54 *quick sense* (1) swift intelligence, (2) lively sensuality   57 *motive* moving
part   59 *coasting welcome* sidelong encouragement   60 *tables* tablets   61
ticklish (1) inquisitive, (2) prurient   61–63 *Set . . . game* enter them in the
list as sluts to be taken as opportunity determines, and as whores   65 *state*
governing body   65–66 *What . . . commands* what reward will go to the victor   66–67 *Or . . . known* do you intend to declare a victor   67 *Will you* do
you intend   68 *edge of all extremity* i.e., without any limitation   69 *Pursue*
fight; *divided* separated   70 *voice* authority; *order of the field* rule of combat

AGAMEMNON   Which way would Hector have it?

AENEAS

72   He cares not; he'll obey conditions.

ACHILLES

73   'Tis done like Hector, but securely done,

74   A little proudly, and great deal misprising
The knight opposed.

AENEAS   If not Achilles, sir,
What is your name?

ACHILLES   If not Achilles, nothing.

AENEAS

Therefore Achilles; but, whate'er, know this:

78   In the extremity of great and little,
Valor and pride excel themselves in Hector,

80   The one almost as infinite as all,
The other blank as nothing. Weigh him well,

82   And that which looks like pride is courtesy.

83   This Ajax is half made of Hector's blood,
In love whereof half Hector stays at home;
Half heart, half hand, half Hector comes to seek
This blended knight, half Trojan, and half Greek.

ACHILLES

87   A maiden battle, then? O, I perceive you.
[Enter Diomedes.]

AGAMEMNON

Here is Sir Diomed. Go, gentle knight,
Stand by our Ajax. As you and Lord Aeneas

90   Consent upon the order of their fight,
So be it; either to the uttermost,

92   Or else a breath. The combatants being kin

---

72 *obey conditions* accept any terms of combat   73 *securely* overconfidently
74 *misprising* underestimating   78–81 *In . . . nothing* i.e., courage and pride
are opposite at the extremes of greatness and smallness in Hector, his courage
being immeasurable and his pride nonexistent   82 *courtesy* fitting dignity
83 *Hector's blood* i.e., Hesione is Hector's aunt and Ajax's mother   87
maiden bloodless; *perceive* understand   90 *Consent* agree; *order* rules   92 *a
breath* an exercise

Half stints their strife before their strokes begin.   93
   [Ajax and Hector enter the lists.]
[ULYSSES
  They are opposed already.]
AGAMEMNON
  What Trojan is that same that looks so heavy?   95
ULYSSES
  The youngest son of Priam, a true knight,
  Not yet mature, yet matchless, firm of word,
  Speaking in deeds and deedless in his tongue,   98
  Not soon provoked, nor being provoked soon calmed;
  His heart and hand both open and both free,   100
  For what he has he gives, what thinks, he shows;   101
  Yet gives he not till judgment guide his bounty,
  Nor dignifies an impare thought with breath;   103
  Manly as Hector, but more dangerous,
  For Hector, in his blaze of wrath, subscribes   105
  To tender objects, but he in heat of action
  Is more vindicative than jealous love.   107
  They call him Troilus, and on him erect
  A second hope as fairly built as Hector.
  Thus says Aeneas, one that knows the youth   *110*
  Even to his inches, and with private soul   111
  Did in great Ilion thus translate him to me.   112
    Alarum. [Hector and Ajax fight.]
AGAMEMNON
  They are in action.
NESTOR
  Now, Ajax, hold thine own!
TROILUS   Hector, thou sleep'st; awake
  thee!
AGAMEMNON
  His blows are well disposed. There, Ajax!   115

---

93 *stints* limits **95** *heavy* sad **98** *deedless . . . tongue* not boastful **100** *free* generous **101** *what thinks* what he thinks **103** *impare* unworthy **105–6** *subscribes . . . objects* gives quarter to the defenseless **107** *vindicative* vindictive **111** *with private soul* in confidence **112** *translate* expound **115** *disposed* placed

DIOMEDES
  You must no more.
      Trumpets cease.
AENEAS   Princes, enough, so please you.
AJAX
  I am not warm yet. Let us fight again.
DIOMEDES
  As Hector pleases.
HECTOR   Why, then will I no more.
  Thou art, great lord, my father's sister's son,
120 A cousin-german to great Priam's seed.
  The obligation of our blood forbids
122 A gory emulation 'twixt us twain.
123 Were thy commixtion Greek and Trojan so
  That thou couldst say, "This hand is Grecian all,
  And this is Trojan; the sinews of this leg
  All Greek, and this all Troy; my mother's blood
127 Runs on the dexter cheek, and this sinister
128 Bounds in my father's," by Jove multipotent,
129 Thou shouldst not bear from me a Greekish member
130 Wherein my sword had not impressure made
131 [Of our rank feud.] But the just gods gainsay
  That any drop thou borrowed'st from thy mother,
133 My sacred aunt, should by my mortal sword
  Be drained! Let me embrace thee, Ajax.
135 By him that thunders, thou hast lusty arms!
  Hector would have them fall upon him thus.
  Cousin, all honor to thee!
AJAX   I thank thee, Hector.
  Thou art too gentle and too free a man.
  I came to kill thee, cousin, and bear hence
140 A great addition earnèd in thy death.

_____

120 *cousin-german . . . seed* cousin   122 *gory emulation* bloody contest   123 *commixtion* mixture   127 *dexter* right; *sinister* left   128 *multipotent* all-powerful   129 *member* limb   130 *impressure* mark, imprint   131 *rank feud* violent war   133 *mortal* deadly   135 *him that thunders* Zeus   140 *addition* title of honor

HECTOR

  Not Neoptolemus so mirable,   141
  On whose bright crest Fame with her loud'st "Oyez"   142
  Cries, "This is he!" could promise to himself   143
  A thought of added honor torn from Hector.

AENEAS

  There is expectance here from both the sides,   145
  What further you will do.

HECTOR   We'll answer it:
  The issue is embracement. Ajax, farewell.   147

AJAX

  If I might in entreaties find success –
  As seld I have the chance – I would desire   149
  My famous cousin to our Grecian tents.   *150*

DIOMEDES

  'Tis Agamemnon's wish, and great Achilles
  Doth long to see unarmed the valiant Hector.

HECTOR

  Aeneas, call my brother Troilus to me,
  And signify this loving interview   154
  To the expecters of our Trojan part.   155
  Desire them home. *[To Ajax]* Give me thy hand, my   156
    cousin;
  I will go eat with thee and see your knights.
    [Agamemnon and the rest approach them.]

AJAX

  Great Agamemnon comes to meet us here.

HECTOR

  The worthiest of them tell me name by name;
  But for Achilles, mine own searching eyes   *160*
  Shall find him by his large and portly size.   161

---

141 *Neoptolemus* Achilles' son (hence also Achilles); *mirable* wonderful 142
crest shield; *Oyez* (heraldic cry preceding a proclamation) 143 *This is he* i.e.,
this is the man 143–44 *could . . . Hector* could count on winning honor from
Hector 145 *expectance* desire to know 147 *issue* outcome 149 *seld* seldom 154 *signify* inform 155 *To . . . part* to Trojans waiting for news 156
Desire them home ask them to return home 161 *portly* stately

AGAMEMNON

  Worthy all arms, *[Embraces him.]* as welcome as to one
  That would be rid of such an enemy –
  [But that's no welcome. Understand more clear,
165 What's past and what's to come is strewed with husks
  And formless ruin of oblivion;
167 But in this extant moment, faith and troth,
168 Strained purely from all hollow bias-drawing,
  Bids thee, with most divine integrity,]
170 From heart of very heart, great Hector, welcome.

HECTOR

171 I thank thee, most imperious Agamemnon.

AGAMEMNON *[To Troilus]*

  My well-famed lord of Troy, no less to you.

MENELAUS

  Let me confirm my princely brother's greeting.
174 You brace of warlike brothers, welcome hither.

HECTOR

  Who must we answer?

AENEAS   The noble Menelaus.

HECTOR

176 O, you, my lord? By Mars his gauntlet, thanks!
177 Mock not that I affect th' untraded oath;
178 Your quondam wife swears still by Venus' glove.
  She's well, but bade me not commend her to you.

MENELAUS

180 Name her not now, sir; she's a deadly theme.

HECTOR

  O, pardon! I offend.

NESTOR

  I have, thou gallant Trojan, seen thee oft,

165–66 *is strewed . . . oblivion* i.e., is littered with empty, disintegrating remnants of greatness en route to being forgotten 167 *extant* present; *troth* truth 168 *Strained . . . bias-drawing* from which all hypocrisies and indirect courses, like the biased trajectory of a bowling ball, have been strained out 171 *imperious* powerful, regal 174 *brace* pair 176 *Mars his gauntlet* the leather glove of Mars, god of war 177 *Mock . . . oath* i.e., don't mock me for affectation in using this newly minted oath 178 *quondam* former

Laboring for destiny, make cruel way   183
Through ranks of Greekish youth, and I have seen thee,
As hot as Perseus, spur thy Phrygian steed,   185
Despising many forfeits and subduements,   186
When thou hast hung thy advancèd sword i' th' air,   187
Not letting it decline on the declined,   188
That I have said to some my standers-by,
"Lo, Jupiter is yonder, dealing life!"   190
And I have seen thee pause and take thy breath,
When that a ring of Greeks have hemmed thee in,
Like an Olympian wrestling. This have I seen,
But this thy countenance, still locked in steel,   194
I never saw till now. I knew thy grandsire,   195
And once fought with him. He was a soldier good,
But, by great Mars, the captain of us all,
Never like thee. Let an old man embrace thee;
And, worthy warrior, welcome to our tents.

AENEAS
'Tis the old Nestor.   *200*

HECTOR
Let me embrace thee, good old chronicle,   201
That hast so long walked hand in hand with time.
Most reverend Nestor, I am glad to clasp thee.   203

NESTOR
I would my arms could match thee in contention,   204
[As they contend with thee in courtesy.]

HECTOR
I would they could.

NESTOR
Ha!
By this white beard, I'd fight with thee tomorrow.

---

183 *Laboring for destiny* doing the work of fate by killing those destined to die   185 *Phrygian steed* Pegasus, the flying horse on which Perseus rode   186 *Despising . . . subduements* scorning to kill many, already vanquished, whose lives were forfeit   187 *advancèd* upraised   188 *decline* fall; *declined* those already defeated   190 *dealing* giving   194 *still* always   195 *grandsire* grandfather   201 *chronicle* i.e., living history   203 *reverend* respected   204 *contention* combat

Well, welcome, welcome. I have seen the time –

ULYSSES

210 I wonder now how yonder city stands,
211 When we have here her base and pillar by us.

HECTOR

212 I know your favor, Lord Ulysses, well.
Ah, sir, there's many a Greek and Trojan dead,
Since first I saw yourself and Diomed
In Ilion, on your Greekish embassy.

ULYSSES

Sir, I foretold you then what would ensue.
My prophecy is but half his journey yet,
218 For yonder walls, that pertly front your town,
219 Yon towers, whose wanton tops do buss the clouds,
220 Must kiss their own feet.

HECTOR   I must not believe you.

221 There they stand yet, and modestly I think,
The fall of every Phrygian stone will cost
A drop of Grecian blood. The end crowns all,
And that old common arbitrator, Time,
Will one day end it.

ULYSSES   So to him we leave it.
Most gentle and most valiant Hector, welcome.
227 After the general, I beseech you next
To feast with me and see me at my tent.

ACHILLES

I shall forestall thee, Lord Ulysses, thou!
230 Now, Hector, I have fed mine eyes on thee;
I have with exact view perused thee, Hector,
232 And quoted joint by joint.

HECTOR   Is this Achilles?

ACHILLES

I am Achilles.

---

211 *her base and pillar* i.e., Hector   212 *favor* face   218 *pertly* boldly   219
buss kiss   221 *modestly* without exaggeration   227 *general* group   232
quoted examined

HECTOR
   Stand fair, I prithee. Let me look on thee.   234
ACHILLES
   Behold thy fill.
HECTOR   Nay, I have done already.
ACHILLES
   Thou art too brief. I will the second time,
   As I would buy thee, view thee limb by limb.
HECTOR
   O, like a book of sport thou'lt read me o'er;   238
   But there's more in me than thou understand'st.
   Why dost thou so oppress me with thine eye?   240
ACHILLES
   Tell me, you heavens, in which part of his body
   Shall I destroy him? Whether there, or there, or there?
   That I may give the local wound a name,
   And make distinct the very breach whereout
   Hector's great spirit flew. Answer me, heavens!
HECTOR
   It would discredit the blessed gods, proud man,
   To answer such a question. Stand again.
   Think'st thou to catch my life so pleasantly   248
   As to prenominate in nice conjecture   249
   Where thou wilt hit me dead?   *250*
ACHILLES   I tell thee, yea.
HECTOR
   Wert thou an oracle to tell me so,
   I'd not believe thee. Henceforth guard thee well,
   For I'll not kill thee there, nor there, nor there,
   But, by the forge that stithied Mars his helm,   254
   I'll kill thee everywhere, yea, o'er and o'er.
   You wisest Grecians, pardon me this brag;
   His insolence draws folly from my lips.

---

234 *fair* in plain view **238** *book of sport* hunting manual **240** *oppress . . .
eye* stare intimidatingly **248** *pleasantly* jokingly **249** *prenominate* name in
advance; *nice* precise **254** *stithied* forged; *helm* helmet

But I'll endeavor deeds to match these words,
259 Or may I never –

AJAX   Do not chafe thee, cousin.
260 And you, Achilles, let these threats alone,
Till accident or purpose bring you to't.
You may have every day enough of Hector,
263 If you have stomach. The general state, I fear,
264 Can scarce entreat you to be odd with him.

HECTOR   *[To Achilles]*
I pray you, let us see you in the field.
266 We have had pelting wars since you refused
The Grecians' cause.

ACHILLES   Dost thou entreat me, Hector?
268 Tomorrow do I meet thee, fell as death;
Tonight all friends.

HECTOR   Thy hand upon that match.

AGAMEMNON
270 First, all you peers of Greece, go to my tent;
271 There in the full convive we. Afterwards,
As Hector's leisure and your bounties shall
273 Concur together, severally entreat him
To taste your bounties. Let the trumpets blow,
That this great soldier may his welcome know.
                    Exeunt [all except Troilus and Ulysses].

TROILUS
My Lord Ulysses, tell me, I beseech you,
277 In what place of the field doth Calchas keep?

ULYSSES
At Menelaus' tent, most princely Troilus.
There Diomed doth feast with him tonight,
280 Who neither looks upon the heaven nor earth,
281 But gives all gaze and bent of amorous view

----

259 *chafe thee* get enraged   263 *stomach* (1) courage, (2) appetite; *general
state* Greek council of war   264 *odd* at odds   266 *pelting* paltry   268 *fell*
fierce   271 *convive* feast   273 *severally* separately   277 *keep* lodge   281
bent inclination

On the fair Cressid.

TROILUS
Shall I, sweet lord, be bound to thee so much,
After we part from Agamemnon's tent,
To bring me thither?

ULYSSES   You shall command me, sir.
As gentle tell me, of what honor was   286
This Cressida in Troy? Had she no lover there
That wails her absence?

TROILUS
O, sir, to such as boasting show their scars
A mock is due. Will you walk on, my lord?   290
She was beloved, she loved; she is, and doth:
But still sweet love is food for fortune's tooth. *Exeunt.*

                              *

∾ **V.1** *Enter Achilles and Patroclus.*

ACHILLES
I'll heat his blood with Greekish wine tonight,
Which with my scimitar I'll cool tomorrow.   2
Patroclus, let us feast him to the height.

PATROCLUS
Here comes Thersites.
        Enter Thersites.

ACHILLES   How now, thou cur of envy!
Thou crusty batch of nature, what's the news?   5

THERSITES   Why, thou picture of what thou seemest, and   6
    idol of idiot-worshipers, here's a letter for thee.

ACHILLES   From whence, fragment?

THERSITES   Why, thou full dish of fool, from Troy.   9
        [Achilles reads.]

---

286 *As gentle* as courteously
    V.1 Before Achilles' tent 2 *scimitar* curved sword 5 *crusty* scabby,
rough, cantankerous; *batch of nature* quantity (in baking) of corrupt nature
6 *picture* simulacrum 9 *dish of fool* bowl of foolishness

10   PATROCLUS   Who keeps the tent now?

11   THERSITES   The surgeon's box or the patient's wound.

12   PATROCLUS   Well said, adversity, and what need these tricks?

THERSITES   Prithee, be silent, boy. I profit not by thy
15   talk. Thou art said to be Achilles' male varlet.

PATROCLUS   Male varlet, you rogue! What's that?

THERSITES   Why, his masculine whore. Now, the rotten
18   diseases of the south, the guts-griping, ruptures, ca-
19   tarrhs, loads o' gravel in the back, lethargies, cold
20   palsies, raw eyes, dirt-rotten livers, wheezing lungs,
21   bladders full of imposthume, sciaticas, limekilns i' th'
22   palm, incurable boneache, and the riveled fee simple of
23   the tetter, and the like, take and take again such preposterous discoveries!

PATROCLUS   Why, thou damnable box of envy, thou,
what means thou to curse thus?

THERSITES   Do I curse thee?

28   PATROCLUS   Why, no, you ruinous butt, you whoreson
29   indistinguishable cur, no.

30   THERSITES   No? Why art thou then exasperate, thou idle
31   immaterial skein of sleave silk, thou green sarcenet flap
32   for a sore eye, thou tassel of a prodigal's purse, thou?
Ah, how the poor world is pestered with such water
34   flies, diminutives of nature.

---

10 *Who . . . now* who is occupying Achilles' tent now (i.e., Achilles can no longer be taunted for keeping to his tent)   11 *The . . . wound* (Patroclus puns on *tent* as a probe for cleaning out wounds)   12 *adversity* perverse or contrary one   15 *male varlet* manservant (already implying sexual servitude)   18 *guts-griping* gut-wrenching spasms; *ruptures* hernias   18–19 *catarrhs* respiratory congestion   19 *loads . . . back* kidney stones; *lethargies* ailments producing torpor   19–20 *cold palsies* paralysis   21 *imposthume* abscesses; *sciaticas* acute aches sometimes associated with venereal disease; *limekilns* burnings   22 *riveled* wrinkled; *fee simple* possession   23 *tetter* skin lesions (ringworm?)   23–24 *preposterous discoveries* perverse or unnatural manifestations (possibly associated by Thersites with anal intercourse)   28 *ruinous butt* dilapidated cask (possibly implying "buttock"); *whoreson* bastard   29 *indistinguishable* shapeless, malformed   31 *sleave silk* silken thread; *sarcenet flap* silk dressing   32 *prodigal's* wastrel's   34 *diminutives* tiny creatures

PATROCLUS   Out, gall!   35
THERSITES   Finch egg!
ACHILLES
  My sweet Patroclus, I am thwarted quite
  From my great purpose in tomorrow's battle.
  Here is a letter from Queen Hecuba,
  A token from her daughter, my fair love,   40
  Both taxing me and gaging me to keep   41
  An oath that I have sworn. I will not break it.
  Fall Greeks, fail fame, honor or go or stay,   43
  My major vow lies here; this I'll obey.
  Come, come, Thersites, help to trim my tent;
  This night in banqueting must all be spent.
  Away, Patroclus!   *Exit [with Patroclus].*
THERSITES   With too much blood and too little brain,
  these two may run mad; but if with too much brain
  and too little blood they do, I'll be a curer of madmen. 50
  Here's Agamemnon, an honest fellow enough, and one
  that loves quails, but he has not so much brain as ear   52
  wax. And the goodly transformation of Jupiter there,   53
  his brother, the bull – the primitive statue and oblique 54
  memorial of cuckolds; a thrifty shoeing horn in a   55
  chain, hanging at his brother's leg – to what form but   56
  that he is should wit larded with malice and malice
  farced with wit turn him to? To an ass, were nothing;   58
  he is both ass and ox. To an ox, were nothing; he is
  both ox and ass. To be a dog, a mule, a cat, a fitchew, a 60
  toad, a lizard, an owl, a puttock, or a herring without a 61
  roe, I would not care; but to be Menelaus! I would con-

---

35 *gall* i.e., prickly or bitter troublemaker 40 *her daughter* Polyxena 41
taxing censuring; *gaging me* binding me to a promise 43 *or . . . or* either . . .
or 52 *quails* prostitutes 53 *goodly . . . Jupiter* (Jupiter transformed himself
into a bull to seduce Europa) 54 *his brother* i.e., Menelaus, the absurdly
horned cuckold 54 *primitive statue* prototype 54–55 *oblique memorial*
distorted image (of *Jupiter*) 55 *thrifty* cheap 55–56 *in a chain* suspended
by a chain from the leg 56–58 *to what . . . to* into what image but his own
should wit basted with malice and malice stuffed with wit turn him 58
farced stuffed 60 *fitchew* polecat 61 *puttock* kite

spire against destiny. Ask me not what I would be, if I
64   were not Thersites, for I care not to be the louse of a
65   lazar, so I were not Menelaus. Hey-day, sprites and
fires!

> *Enter Agamemnon, Ulysses, Nestor, [Hector, Ajax,*
> *Troilus, Menelaus,] and Diomedes, with lights.*

AGAMEMNON
We go wrong, we go wrong.

AJAX   No, yonder 'tis –
There, where we see the lights.

HECTOR   I trouble you.

AJAX
No, not a whit.

ULYSSES   Here comes himself to guide you.
> *[Enter Achilles.]*

ACHILLES
70   Welcome, brave Hector. Welcome, princes all.

AGAMEMNON
So now, fair prince of Troy, I bid good night.
Ajax commands the guard to tend on you.

HECTOR
73   Thanks and good night to the Greeks' general.

MENELAUS
Good night, my lord.

HECTOR
Good night, sweet Lord Menelaus.

76 THERSITES   *[Aside]* Sweet draught! "Sweet," quoth a!
77   Sweet sink, sweet sewer.

ACHILLES
Good night and welcome both at once, to those
That go or tarry.

80 AGAMEMNON   Good night.
> *Exeunt Agamemnon [and] Menelaus.*

---

64 *I care not to be* I wouldn't mind being   **65** *lazar* leper   **65–66** *sprites and*
fires (Thersites pretends that the light of the approaching torches is ghostly)
73 *Greeks' general* (1) Agamemnon, (2) all the Greeks   **76** *draught* privy   **77**
sink cesspool

ACHILLES

　　Old Nestor tarries, and you too, Diomed,
　　Keep Hector company an hour or two.

DIOMEDES

　　I cannot, lord. I have important business,
　　The tide whereof is now. Good night, great Hector.　　84

HECTOR

　　Give me your hand.

ULYSSES　　*[Aside to Troilus]*

　　Follow his torch; he goes to Calchas' tent.
　　I'll keep you company.

TROILUS　　*[Aside to Ulysses]*

　　Sweet sir, you honor me.

HECTOR　　　　　　　　　　　And so, good night.
　　　　　　[Exeunt Diomedes, then Ulysses and Troilus.]

ACHILLES

　　Come, come, enter my tent.
　　　　　　　　Exeunt [Achilles, Hector, Ajax, and Nestor].

THERSITES　　That same Diomed's a false-hearted rogue, a　　90
　　most unjust knave. I will no more trust him when he
　　leers than I will a serpent when he hisses. He will spend　　92
　　his mouth and promise like Brabbler the hound, but
　　when he performs, astronomers foretell it; it is prodi-　　94
　　gious, there will come some change. The sun borrows　　95
　　of the moon when Diomed keeps his word. I will rather
　　leave to see Hector than not to dog him. They say he　　97
　　keeps a Trojan drab, and uses the traitor Calchas' tent.　　98
　　I'll after – nothing but lechery! All incontinent varlets!
　　　　　　　　　　　　　　　　　　　　　Exit.

*

---

84 *tide* time　**92–93** *spend . . . hound* i.e., bay as if closing in for the kill like
Brabbler the hunting dog (the name implying a troublemaking loudmouth)
94 *performs* i.e., keeps his word (as distinct from promising); *astronomers
foretell it* i.e., it is a rare, wondrous event, promising momentous change
95–96 *borrows of the moon* reflects the light of the moon rather than being
reflected by it (i.e., the order of nature is reversed)　**97** *leave to see* miss seeing; *dog* follow　**98** *drab* whore

∽ **V.2** *Enter Diomed.*

DIOMEDES   What, are you up here, ho? Speak.

CALCHAS   *[Within]* Who calls?

DIOMEDES   Diomed. Calchas, I think? Where's your daughter?

CALCHAS   *[Within]* She comes to you.
      Enter Troilus and Ulysses [; after them Thersites].

ULYSSES   *[To Troilus, aside]*
6   Stand where the torch may not discover us.
      Enter Cressid.

TROILUS   *[To Ulysses, aside]*
   Cressid comes forth to him.

DIOMEDES   How now, my charge!

CRESSIDA
   Now, my sweet guardian! Hark, a word with you.
      [Whispers.]

TROILUS   *[Aside]* Yea, so familiar?

10   ULYSSES   *[To Troilus, aside]* She will sing any man at first sight.

THERSITES   *[Aside]* And any man may sing her, if he can
13   take her cliff. She's noted.

DIOMEDES   Will you remember?

CRESSIDA   Remember? Yes.

DIOMEDES   Nay, but do, then,
   And let your mind be coupled with your words.

TROILUS   *[Aside]* What should she remember?

19   ULYSSES   *[To Troilus, aside]* List!

CRESSIDA
20   Sweet honey Greek, tempt me no more to folly.

THERSITES   *[Aside]* Roguery!

DIOMEDES
   Nay, then –

V.2 Before Calchas's tent   **6** *discover* reveal   **10–11** *sing . . . at first sight* (1) sing on first encounter, (2) sight-read any man she meets   **13** *cliff* (1) musical clef, (2) genital cleft; *noted* notorious (punning on musical notation)   **19** *List* listen

CRESSIDA   I'll tell you what –
DIOMEDES
    Foh, foh! come, tell a pin. You are forsworn.   23
CRESSIDA
    In faith, I cannot. What would you have me do?
THERSITES   *[Aside]* A juggling trick – to be secretly open.   25
DIOMEDES
    What did you swear you would bestow on me?
CRESSIDA
    I prithee, do not hold me to mine oath;
    Bid me do anything but that, sweet Greek.
DIOMEDES   Good night.
TROILUS   *[Aside]* Hold, patience!   30
ULYSSES   *[To Troilus, aside]* How now, Trojan?
CRESSIDA   Diomed –
DIOMEDES
    No, no, good night. I'll be your fool no more.
TROILUS   *[Aside]*
    Thy better must.
CRESSIDA   Hark, a word in your ear.
TROILUS   *[Aside]*
    O plague and madness!
ULYSSES   *[To Troilus, aside]*
    You are moved, prince. Let us depart, I pray you,
    Lest your displeasure should enlarge itself   37
    To wrathful terms. This place is dangerous,
    The time right deadly. I beseech you, go.
TROILUS   *[To Ulysses, aside]*
    Behold, I pray you!   40
ULYSSES   *[To Troilus, aside]*
                Nay, good my lord, go off.
    You flow to great distraction. Come, my lord.   41

---

23 *tell a pin* trifle with me (from the trifling nature of pins)   **25** *juggling trick* magical trick; *secretly open* appear chaste yet be sexually willing (bodily available)   **37** *enlarge* (1) increase, (2) let itself go   **41** *flow . . . distraction* are being carried on a tide to madness

TROILUS   *[To Ulysses, aside]*
I prithee, stay.

ULYSSES   *[To Troilus, aside]*
                    You have not patience. Come.

TROILUS   *[To Ulysses, aside]*
I pray you, stay. By hell, and all hell's torments,
I will not speak a word!

DIOMEDES   And so, good night.

CRESSIDA
Nay, but you part in anger.

TROILUS   *[Aside]*   Doth that grieve thee?
O withered truth!

ULYSSES   *[To Troilus, aside]*
                    How now, my lord!

TROILUS   *[To Ulysses, aside]*   By Jove,
I will be patient.

CRESSIDA   Guardian! Why, Greek!

DIOMEDES
48   Foh, foh! adieu; you palter.

CRESSIDA
In faith, I do not. Come hither once again.

ULYSSES   *[To Troilus, aside]*
50   You shake, my lord, at something. Will you go?
You will break out.

TROILUS   *[Aside]*   She strokes his cheek!

ULYSSES   Come, come.

TROILUS   *[To Ulysses, aside]*
Nay, stay. By Jove, I will not speak a word.
53   There is between my will and all offenses
54   A guard of patience. Stay a little while.

55   THERSITES   *[Aside]* How the devil Luxury, with his fat
56   rump and potato finger, tickles these together. Fry,
lechery, fry!

DIOMEDES   But will you, then?

---

48 *palter* trifle   53 *offenses* offensive actions   54 *guard* barrier   55 *Luxury* lechery (personified)   56 *potato finger* (potatoes were believed to be sexually stimulating, but their shape also conjures a coarse, probing finger)   56–57 *Fry . . . fry* burn

CRESSIDA
  In faith, I will, la. Never trust me else.
DIOMEDES
  Give me some token for the surety of it.   60
CRESSIDA
  I'll fetch you one.   *Exit.*
ULYSSES   *[To Troilus, aside]*
  You have sworn patience.   62
TROILUS   *[To Ulysses, aside]* Fear me not, my lord.
  I will not be myself, nor have cognition
  Of what I feel. I am all patience.
      Enter Cressid.
THERSITES   *[Aside]* Now the pledge; now, now, now!
CRESSIDA   Here, Diomed, keep this sleeve.
TROILUS   *[Aside]*
  O beauty, where is thy faith?
ULYSSES   *[To Troilus, aside]*   My lord –
[TROILUS   *[To Ulysses, aside]*
  I will be patient; outwardly I will.]
CRESSIDA
  You look upon that sleeve; behold it well.   69
  He loved me – O false wench! Give't me again.   70
DIOMEDES
  Whose was't?
CRESSIDA   It is no matter, now I have't again.
  I will not meet with you tomorrow night.
  I prithee, Diomed, visit me no more.
THERSITES   *[Aside]* Now she sharpens. Well said, whet-   74
  stone!
DIOMEDES
  I shall have it.
CRESSIDA   What, this?
DIOMEDES   Ay, that.
CRESSIDA
  O, all you gods! O pretty, pretty pledge!

---

62 *Fear me not* i.e., don't be afraid I'll break out   69 *sleeve* (the detachable
sleeve Troilus has given her as a love token)   74 *sharpens* i.e., whets his desire

Thy master now lies thinking in his bed
Of thee and me, and sighs, and takes my glove,

80   And gives memorial dainty kisses to it – *[He snatches
the sleeve.]*

DIOMEDES
As I kiss thee. Nay, do not snatch it from me.

CRESSIDA
He that takes that doth take my heart withal.

DIOMEDES
I had your heart before. This follows it.

TROILUS   *[To Ulysses, aside]*
I did swear patience.

CRESSIDA
You shall not have it, Diomed; faith, you shall not.
I'll give you something else.

DIOMEDES
I will have this. Whose was it?

CRESSIDA   It is no matter.

DIOMEDES
Come, tell me whose it was.

CRESSIDA
'Twas one's that loved me better than you will.

90   But, now you have it, take it.

DIOMEDES   Whose was it?

CRESSIDA

91   By all Diana's waiting women yond,
And by herself, I will not tell you whose.

DIOMEDES
Tomorrow will I wear it on my helm,

94   And grieve his spirit that dares not challenge it.

TROILUS   *[Aside]*
Wert thou the devil, and wor'st it on thy horn,
It should be challenged.

CRESSIDA
Well, well, 'tis done, 'tis past. And yet it is not;

---

91 *Diana's waiting women* i.e., the stars **94** *grieve his spirit* may his spirit
grieve

I will not keep my word.

DIOMEDES   Why then, farewell.
Thou never shalt mock Diomed again.

CRESSIDA
You shall not go. One cannot speak a word   *100*
But it straight starts you.   101

DIOMEDES   I do not like this fooling.

THERSITES   *[Aside]* Nor I, by Pluto; but that that likes   102
not you pleases me best.

DIOMEDES
What, shall I come? The hour?

CRESSIDA   Ay, come – O Jove! – Do come – I shall be
plagued.   106

DIOMEDES   Farewell till then.

CRESSIDA
Good night. I prithee, come.   *[Exit Diomedes.]*
Troilus, farewell. One eye yet looks on thee,
But with my heart the other eye doth see.   *110*
Ah, poor our sex! This fault in us I find,   111
The error of our eye directs our mind.   112
What error leads must err. O, then conclude
Minds swayed by eyes are full of turpitude.   *Exit.*

THERSITES   *[Aside]*
A proof of strength she could not publish more,   115
Unless she say, "My mind is now turned whore."

ULYSSES
All's done, my lord.

TROILUS   It is.

ULYSSES   Why stay we, then?

TROILUS
To make a recordation to my soul   118
Of every syllable that here was spoke.
But if I tell how these two did co-act,   *120*
Shall I not lie in publishing a truth?

---

101 *starts* makes you back off   102 *likes* pleases   106 *plagued* punished
111 *poor our* our poor   112 *error* straying   115 *A proof . . . publish more* i.e.,
she could hardly make the point more strongly   118 *recordation* record

122 Sith yet there is a credence in my heart,
123 An esperance so obstinately strong,
124 That doth invert th' attest of eyes and ears,
125 As if those organs had deceptious functions,
126 Created only to calumniate.
127 Was Cressid here?

ULYSSES   I cannot conjure, Trojan.

TROILUS
She was not, sure.

ULYSSES   Most sure she was.

TROILUS
129 Why, my negation hath no taste of madness.

ULYSSES
130 Nor mine, my lord. Cressid was here but now.

TROILUS
131 Let it not be believed for womanhood!
Think, we had mothers. Do not give advantage
133 To stubborn critics, apt, without a theme
134 For depravation, to square the general sex
135 By Cressid's rule. Rather think this not Cressid.

ULYSSES
What hath she done, prince, that can soil our mothers?

TROILUS
Nothing at all, unless that this were she.

138 THERSITES   *[Aside]* Will a swagger himself out on's own
eyes?

TROILUS
140 This she? No, this is Diomed's Cressida.
If beauty have a soul, this is not she;
142 If souls guide vows, if vows be sanctimonies,

---

122 *credence* belief   123 *esperance* hope   124 *th' attest* testimony   125 *deceptious* deceiving   126 *calumniate* slander   127 *conjure* raise spirits   129 *my . . . madness* my denial does not smack of madness   131 *for womanhood* for the sake of womankind   133 *stubborn critics* implacable, carping misogynists; *apt* ready   133–34 *without . . . depravation* without any specific cause or lacking any other topic for slander   134 *square* align, measure   135 *rule* norm, yardstick   138–39 *swagger . . . eyes* bluster his way out of what he has seen   142 *sanctimonies* sacred bonds

If sanctimony be the gods' delight,   143
If there be rule in unity itself,   144
This was not she. O madness of discourse,
That cause sets up with and against itself;   146
Bifold authority, where reason can revolt   147
Without perdition, and loss assume all reason
Without revolt. This is and is not Cressid.
Within my soul there doth conduce a fight   150
Of this strange nature that a thing inseparate   151
Divides more wider than the sky and earth;
And yet the spacious breadth of this division
Admits no orifice for a point as subtle   154
As Ariachne's broken woof to enter.   155
Instance, O instance, strong as Pluto's gates,   156
Cressid is mine, tied with the bonds of heaven.
Instance, O instance, strong as heaven itself,
The bonds of heaven are slipped, dissolved, and loosed,
And with another knot, five-finger-tied,   160
The fractions of her faith, orts of her love,   161
The fragments, scraps, the bits, and greasy relics
Of her o'ereaten faith, are bound to Diomed.   163

ULYSSES
May worthy Troilus be half attached   164
With that which here his passion doth express?

---

143 *sanctimony* holiness   144 *rule in unity* i.e., rule of indivisibility and noncontradiction in unity (Cressida being one, not two)   146 *That . . . itself* that can make a case for and against its own reasoning   147 *Bifold* double; *where reason can revolt* where reason can revolt against itself without losing its own character, and where unreason can take on the appearance of rationality without contradiction   150 *conduce* occur   151 *inseparate* indivisible   154 *Admits* includes, contains   155 *Ariachne* (Ariachne is Shakespeare's coinage, combining Ariadne, who led Theseus out of the Minotaur's labyrinth with a silken thread, and Arachne, a superlative weaver whose tapestry the vindictive Minerva destroyed, and whom Minerva turned into a spider); *broken woof* i.e., a filament or thread   156 *Instance* evidence   160 *five-finger-tied* i.e., by holding hands with Diomed or perhaps tied by profane human hands, not heavenly ones   161 *fractions* fragments; *orts* leftovers   163 *o'ereaten* nibbled all around   164 *half attached* half as much attached

TROILUS

166 Ay, Greek, and that shall be divulgèd well
167 In characters as red as Mars his heart
     Inflamed with Venus. Never did young man fancy
     With so eternal and so fixed a soul.
170 Hark, Greek: as much as I do Cressid love,
171 So much by weight hate I her Diomed.
     That sleeve is mine that he'll bear on his helm;
173 Were it a casque composed by Vulcan's skill,
174 My sword should bite it. Not the dreadful spout
     Which shipmen do the hurricano call,
176 Constringed in mass by the almighty sun,
     Shall dizzy with more clamor Neptune's ear
178 In his descent than shall my prompted sword
     Falling on Diomed.

180 THERSITES *[Aside]* He'll tickle it for his concupy.

TROILUS

     O Cressid! O false Cressid! False, false, false!
     Let all untruths stand by thy stainèd name,
     And they'll seem glorious.

ULYSSES   O, contain yourself;
     Your passion draws ears hither.

          Enter Aeneas.

AENEAS *[To Troilus]*
     I have been seeking you this hour, my lord.
186 Hector, by this, is arming him in Troy.
     Ajax, your guard, stays to conduct you home.

TROILUS
188 Have with you, prince. My courteous lord, adieu.
     Farewell, revolted fair – and Diomed,
190 Stand fast, and wear a castle on thy head!

ULYSSES
     I'll bring you to the gates.

---

166 *divulgèd* revealed, expressed 167 *characters* letters 171 *So . . . weight*
in equal measure 173 *casque* helmet 174 *spout* waterspout 176 *Constringed* pulled together 178 *prompted* motivated 180 *tickle* i.e., rain
blows; *concupy* (1) concubine, (2) concupiscence (lust) 186 *by this* by now
188 *Have with you* I'm ready to go with you

TROILUS
Accept distracted thanks.
                    Exeunt Troilus, Aeneas, and Ulysses.
THERSITES   Would I could meet that rogue Diomed. I
would croak like a raven; I would bode, I would bode.   194
Patroclus will give me anything for the intelligence of   195
this whore. The parrot will not do more for an almond   196
than he for a commodious drab. Lechery, lechery, still   197
wars and lechery; nothing else holds fashion. A burning
devil take them!   *Exit.*

                         *

∾ **V.3** *Enter Hector [armed] and Andromache.*

ANDROMACHE
When was my lord so much ungently tempered,   1
To stop his ears against admonishment?
Unarm, unarm, and do not fight today.
HECTOR
You train me to offend you. Get you in.   4
By all the everlasting gods, I'll go.
ANDROMACHE
My dreams will sure prove ominous to the day.
HECTOR
No more, I say.
      Enter Cassandra.
CASSANDRA   Where is my brother Hector?
ANDROMACHE
Here, sister, armed and bloody in intent.
Consort with me in loud and dear petition;   9
Pursue we him on knees, for I have dreamed   10
Of bloody turbulence, and this whole night
Hath nothing been but shapes and forms of slaughter.

---

194 *bode* portend doom 195 *intelligence of* information about 196
parrot . . . almond (parrots were believed to love almonds) 197 *commodious
drab* accommodating whore
   V.3 Before Priam's palace 1 *ungently tempered* impolite, ill-natured 4
train induce 9 *Consort* join; *dear petition* earnest plea

CASSANDRA
  O, 'tis true.
HECTOR   Ho! Bid my trumpet sound.
CASSANDRA
  No notes of sally, for the heavens, sweet brother.
HECTOR
  Be gone, I say. The gods have heard me swear.
CASSANDRA
16 The gods are deaf to hot and peevish vows.
  They are polluted off'rings, more abhorred
18 Than spotted livers in the sacrifice.
ANDROMACHE
  O, be persuaded! Do not count it holy
20 [To hurt by being just. It is as lawful,
21 For we would give much, to use violent thefts,
  And rob in the behalf of charity.
CASSANDRA]
  It is the purpose that makes strong the vow,
24 But vows to every purpose must not hold.
  Unarm, sweet Hector.
HECTOR   Hold you still, I say.
26 Mine honor keeps the weather of my fate.
27 Life every man holds dear, but the dear man
  Holds honor far more precious-dear than life.
     Enter Troilus [armed].
  How now, young man, mean'st thou to fight today?
ANDROMACHE
30 Cassandra, call my father to persuade. *Exit Cassandra.*
HECTOR
  No, faith, young Troilus; doff thy harness, youth.
32 I am today i' th' vein of chivalry.
33 Let grow thy sinews till their knots be strong,

---

16 *peevish* willful, perverse 18 *spotted* diseased 20 *just* faithful (to a vow)
21 *For* because 24 *hold* be held sacred 26 *keeps the weather of* keeps to the
windward of (i.e., takes precedence over) 27 *dear* worthy 30 *father* Priam
(Andromache's father-in-law) 32 *i' th' vein* in the mood; *chivalry* fighting
33 *knots* ligaments

And tempt not yet the brushes of the war.   34
Unarm thee, go, and doubt thou not, brave boy,
I'll stand today for thee and me and Troy.

TROILUS
Brother, you have a vice of mercy in you,
Which better fits a lion than a man.

HECTOR
What vice is that? Good Troilus, chide me for it.

TROILUS
When many times the captive Grecian falls,   40
Even in the fan and wind of your fair sword,   41
You bid them rise and live.

HECTOR
O, 'tis fair play.

TROILUS   Fool's play, by heaven, Hector.

HECTOR
How now, how now?

TROILUS   For th' love of all the gods,
Let's leave the hermit pity with our mother,   45
And when we have our armors buckled on,
The venomed vengeance ride upon our swords,
Spur them to ruthful work, rein them from ruth.   48

HECTOR
Fie, savage, fie!   49

TROILUS   Hector, then 'tis wars.

HECTOR
Troilus, I would not have you fight today.   50

TROILUS
Who should withhold me?
Not fate, obedience, nor the hand of Mars
Beck'ning with fiery truncheon my retire;   53
Not Priamus and Hecuba on knees,

---

34 *brushes* encounters   41 *fan and wind* i.e., the mere wind produced by his
sword stroke   45 *hermit* i.e., which should be in a solitary place apart from
the battle   48 *ruthful* causing to be pitied; *ruth* pity   49 *then 'tis wars* (1)
that's war, (2) that's when it really is war   53 *truncheon* staff used to signal
the end of combat at a tourney

55   Their eyes o'ergallèd with recourse of tears;
        Nor you, my brother, with your true sword drawn,
        Opposed to hinder me, should stop my way,
58   [But by my ruin.]
            Enter Priam and Cassandra.
        CASSANDRA
        Lay hold upon him, Priam, hold him fast;
60   He is thy crutch. Now if thou lose thy stay,
        Thou on him leaning, and all Troy on thee,
        Fall all together.
        PRIAM   Come, Hector, come; go back.
        Thy wife hath dreamt, thy mother hath had visions,
        Cassandra doth foresee, and I myself
65   Am like a prophet suddenly enrapt
        To tell thee that this day is ominous:
        Therefore, come back.
        HECTOR   Aeneas is afield;
68   And I do stand engaged to many Greeks,
        Even in the faith of valor, to appear
70   This morning to them.
        PRIAM   Ay, but thou shalt not go.
        HECTOR
        I must not break my faith.
        You know me dutiful; therefore, dear sir,
73   Let me not shame respect, but give me leave
        To take that course by your consent and voice,
        Which you do here forbid me, royal Priam.
        CASSANDRA
        O Priam, yield not to him!
        ANDROMACHE   Do not, dear father.
        HECTOR
        Andromache, I am offended with you.
        Upon the love you bear me, get you in.
                            Exit Andromache.

---

55 *o'ergallèd* inflamed; *recourse of* having recourse to   58 *ruin* death   60 *stay*
prop   65 *enrapt* rapt in a prophetic trance   68 *engaged* pledged   73 *shame
respect* bring disgrace by withholding the respect I owe you

TROILUS
   This foolish, dreaming, superstitious girl
   Makes all these bodements.   80
CASSANDRA   O farewell, dear Hector!
   Look, how thou diest; look, how thy eye turns pale;
   Look, how thy wounds do bleed at many vents!
   Hark, how Troy roars, how Hecuba cries out,
   How poor Andromache shrills her dolors forth!   84
   Behold, distraction, frenzy, and amazement,   85
   Like witless antics, one another meet,   86
   And all cry "Hector! Hector's dead! O Hector!"
TROILUS
   Away! Away!
CASSANDRA
   Farewell. Yet, soft: Hector, I take my leave.
   Thou dost thyself and all our Troy deceive.   *[Exit.]*   90
HECTOR
   You are amazed, my liege, at her exclaim.   91
   Go in and cheer the town. We'll forth and fight,
   Do deeds worth praise and tell you them at night.
PRIAM
   Farewell. The gods with safety stand about thee.
         [Exeunt Priam and Hector.] Alarum.
TROILUS
   They are at it, hark! Proud Diomed, believe,
   I come to lose my arm, or win my sleeve.
    Enter Pandarus.
PANDARUS   Do you hear, my lord? Do you hear?
TROILUS   What now?
PANDARUS   Here's a letter come from yond poor girl.
TROILUS   Let me read. *[Reads.]*   100
PANDARUS   A whoreson tisick, a whoreson rascally tisick   101
   so troubles me, and the foolish fortune of this girl, and
   what one thing, what another, that I shall leave you one

---

80 *bodements* ominous prophecies 84 *dolors* griefs 85 *amazement* bemuse-
ment 86 *antics* clowns, grotesque performers (here, mad ones) 91 *amazed*
bewildered, disconcerted 101 *tisick* cough

104   o' these days. And I have a rheum in mine eyes too, and
105   such an ache in my bones that, unless a man were
     cursed, I cannot tell what to think on't. What says she
     there?

TROILUS
     Words, words, mere words, no matter from the heart;
     Th' effect doth operate another way.
       [Tearing the letter]
110   Go, wind to wind, there turn and change together.
     My love with words and errors still she feeds,
112   But edifies another with her deeds.   *Exeunt.*

*

∾ **V.4** *[Alarum.] Excursions. Enter Thersites.*

1 THERSITES   Now they are clapper-clawing one another.
     I'll go look on. That dissembling abominable varlet,
     Diomed, has got that same scurvy doting foolish young
     knave's sleeve of Troy there in his helm. I would fain see
     them meet, that that same young Trojan ass, that loves
     the whore there, might send that Greekish whoremas-
7   terly villain with the sleeve back to the dissembling lux-
8   urious drab, of a sleeveless errand. O' th' t' other side,
9   the policy of those crafty swearing rascals – that stale
10   old mouse-eaten dry cheese, Nestor, and that same
     dog-fox, Ulysses – is not proved worth a blackberry.
12   They set me up, in policy, that mongrel cur, Ajax,
     against that dog of as bad a kind, Achilles. And now is
     the cur Ajax prouder than the cur Achilles, and will not
15   arm today. Whereupon the Grecians begin to proclaim
16   barbarism, and policy grows into an ill opinion.

---

104 *rheum* discharge   105 *ache in my bones* (here, probably a syphilitic symptom)   112 *edifies* builds up, arouses

    V.4 Battlefield   1 *clapper-clawing* clawing, tussling   7–8 *luxurious drab* lecherous whore   8 *sleeveless* fruitless   9 *policy* craftiness, strategy; *crafty swearing* making of deceitful promises   12 *set me up* set up   15–16 *proclaim barbarism* affirm the authority of ignorance   16 *grows into an ill opinion* comes into disrepute

[Enter Diomedes and Troilus.]
Soft! here comes sleeve, and t' other.

TROILUS
Fly not, for shouldst thou take the River Styx,   18
I would swim after.   19

DIOMEDES   Thou dost miscall retire.
I do not fly, but advantageous care   20
Withdrew me from the odds of multitude.   21
Have at thee! *[They fight.]*

THERSITES   Hold thy whore, Grecian! Now for thy
whore, Trojan! Now the sleeve, now the sleeve!
                    [Exeunt Troilus and Diomedes, fighting.]
    Enter Hector.

HECTOR
What art thou, Greek? Art thou for Hector's match?   25
Art thou of blood and honor?   26

THERSITES   No, no. I am a rascal, a scurvy railing knave,
a very filthy rogue.

HECTOR
I do believe thee. Live.   *[Exit.]*

THERSITES   God-a-mercy, that thou wilt believe me; but   30
a plague break thy neck – for frighting me! What's become of the wenching rogues? I think they have swal-
lowed one another. I would laugh at that miracle – yet,
in a sort, lechery eats itself. I'll seek them.   *Exit.*   34

                        *

❧ **V.5** *Enter Diomed and Servant.*

DIOMEDES
Go, go, my servant, take thou Troilus' horse;
Present the fair steed to my Lady Cressid.

---

18 *take . . . Styx* jump into the River Styx to escape into the underworld   **19**
miscall retire misname my deliberate withdrawal a flight   **20** *advantageous
care* prudent exploitation of opportunity   **21** *odds of multitude* overwhelm-
ing odds   **25** *for Hector's match* a match for Hector   **26** *of blood and honor* a
nobleman   **30** *God-a-mercy* thank God   **34** *in a sort* in a way
    V.5 Battlefield

Fellow, commend my service to her beauty;
Tell her I have chastised the amorous Trojan,
And am her knight by proof.
SERVANT   I go, my lord.   *[Exit.]*
    Enter Agamemnon.
AGAMEMNON
    Renew, renew! The fierce Polydamas
    Hath beat down Menon; bastard Margarelon
    Hath Doreus prisoner,
9   And stands colossus-wise, waving his beam,
10 Upon the pashèd corses of the kings
    Epistrophus and Cedius. Polixenes is slain,
    Amphimachus and Thoas deadly hurt,
    Patroclus ta'en or slain, and Palamedes
14 Sore hurt and bruisèd. The dreadful Sagittary
15 Appals our numbers. Haste we, Diomed,
    To reinforcement, or we perish all.
        Enter Nestor [with Soldiers bearing Patroclus' body].
NESTOR
    Go, bear Patroclus' body to Achilles,
    And bid the snail-paced Ajax arm for shame.
                                    [Exeunt Soldiers.]
    There is a thousand Hectors in the field.
20 Now here he fights on Galathe his horse,
    And there lacks work; anon he's there afoot,
22 And there they fly or die, like scalèd sculls
    Before the belching whale; then is he yonder,
24 And there the strawy Greeks, ripe for his edge,
25 Fall down before him, like a mower's swath.
    Here, there, and everywhere, he leaves and takes,
    Dexterity so obeying appetite
    That what he will he does, and does so much

---

9 *beam* huge staff or lance   10 *pashèd corses* battered corpses   14 *dreadful
Sagittary* fearsome centaur (half man, half horse) who aided the Trojans (possible allusion to Hector as well)   15 *Appals our numbers* dismays our army
22 *scalèd sculls* scaly fish (in schools)   24 *strawy* i.e., like corn waiting to be
cut down   25 *swath* row of mown grain

That proof is called impossibility.   29
   Enter Ulysses.

ULYSSES
  O, courage, courage, princes! Great Achilles   30
  Is arming, weeping, cursing, vowing vengeance.
  Patroclus' wounds have roused his drowsy blood,
  Together with his mangled Myrmidons,   33
  That noseless, handless, hacked and chipped, come to
    him,
  Crying on Hector. Ajax hath lost a friend,
  And foams at mouth, and he is armed and at it,
  Roaring for Troilus, who hath done today
  Mad and fantastic execution,
  Engaging and redeeming of himself   39
  With such a careless force and forceless care   40
  As if that luck, in very spite of cunning,   41
  Bade him win all.
    Enter Ajax.

AJAX
  Troilus, thou coward Troilus!   *Exit.*
DIOMEDES   Ay, there, there.
NESTOR
  So, so, we draw together.   *Exit.*
    Enter Achilles.
ACHILLES   Where is this Hector?
  Come, come, thou boy-queller, show thy face;   45
  Know what it is to meet Achilles angry.
  Hector, where's Hector? I will none but Hector.   *Exit.*

✻

---

29 *proof . . . impossibility* i.e., even his proven accomplishments seem impos-
sible   **33** *Myrmidons* (Achilles' followers, mythically descended from a
swarm of ants [Greek *myrmes*]   **39** *Engaging . . . himself* engaging in close
combat and withdrawing to safety   **40** *careless force . . . forceless care* unruf-
fled exertion of strength . . . effortless vigilance   **41–42** *As if . . . all* (1) as if
luck rather than skill enjoined him to win all, (2) as if his luck prevailed over
the skill of his enemies   **45** *boy-queller* boy-killer

∾ **V.6** *Enter Ajax.*

AJAX
Troilus, thou coward Troilus, show thy head.
Enter Diomedes.

DIOMEDES
Troilus, I say, where's Troilus?

AJAX   What wouldst thou?

DIOMEDES
I would correct him.

AJAX
Were I the general, thou shouldst have my office
5   Ere that correction. Troilus, I say! What, Troilus!
Enter Troilus.

TROILUS
O traitor Diomed! Turn thy false face, thou traitor,
And pay thy life thou owest me for my horse.

DIOMEDES
Ha, art thou there?

AJAX
I'll fight with him alone. Stand, Diomed.

DIOMEDES
10   He is my prize. I will not look upon.

TROILUS
11   Come, both you cogging Greeks, have at you both!
[Exeunt, fighting.]
[Enter Hector.]

HECTOR
Yea, Troilus? O, well fought, my youngest brother!
Enter Achilles.

ACHILLES
Now do I see thee. Have at thee, Hector!
[They fight.]

HECTOR
Pause, if thou wilt.

V.6 Battlefield   **5** *Ere that correction* before depriving me of the right to chastise Troilus   **10** *look upon* be a spectator   **11** *cogging* deceitful

ACHILLES
 I do disdain thy courtesy, proud Trojan.   15
 Be happy that my arms are out of use.
 My rest and negligence befriends thee now,
 But thou anon shalt hear of me again;
 Till when, go seek thy fortune.   *Exit.*

HECTOR   Fare thee well:
 I would have been much more a fresher man, 20
 Had I expected thee.
   Enter Troilus.
 How now, my brother!

TROILUS
 Ajax hath ta'en Aeneas! Shall it be?   23
 No, by the flame of yonder glorious heaven,
 He shall not carry him. I'll be ta'en too, 25
 Or bring him off. Fate, hear me what I say! 26
 I reck not though thou end my life today. *Exit.* 27
   Enter one in armor.

HECTOR
 Stand, stand, thou Greek; thou art a goodly mark. 28
 No? Wilt thou not? I like thy armor well;
 I'll frush it and unlock the rivets all, 30
 But I'll be master of it. Wilt thou not, beast, abide?
 Why then, fly on, I'll hunt thee for thy hide.
        Exit [in pursuit].

*

∾ **V.7** *[Enter Achilles with Myrmidons.]*

ACHILLES
 Come here about me, you my Myrmidons;
 Mark what I say. Attend me where I wheel; 2
 Strike not a stroke, but keep yourselves in breath;

---

15 *courtesy* courteous offer of a respite **23** *ta'en* captured **25** *carry* conquer
26 *bring him off* rescue him **27** *reck* care **28** *mark* target **30** *frush* smash
 V.7 Battlefield **2** *Attend* (1) watch me, (2) stick with me; *wheel* circle
around

And when I have the bloody Hector found,
5   Empale him with your weapons round about;
6   In fellest manner execute your arms.
Follow me, sirs, and my proceedings eye.
It is decreed, Hector the great must die.
                              Exit [with Myrmidons].
Enter Thersites, Menelaus, Paris [, the last two
fighting].

THERSITES   The cuckold and the cuckold-maker are at
10   it. Now, bull! Now, dog! 'Loo, Paris, 'loo! Now, my
11   double-horned Spartan! 'Loo, Paris, 'loo! The bull has
12   the game; 'ware horns, ho!
                              Exeunt Paris and Menelaus.
Enter Bastard [Margarelon].

MARGARELON   Turn, slave, and fight.

THERSITES   What art thou?

MARGARELON   A bastard son of Priam's.

THERSITES   I am a bastard too; I love bastards. I am bastard begot, bastard instructed, bastard in mind, bastard
in valor, in everything illegitimate. One bear will not
bite another, and wherefore should one bastard? Take
20   heed, the quarrel's most ominous to us. If the son of a
whore fight for a whore, he tempts judgment. Farewell,
bastard.

MARGARELON   The devil take thee, coward!   *Exit.*

                              *

∾ **V.8** *Enter Hector.*

HECTOR   *[Dragging a Greek in armor]*
1   Most putrefied core, so fair without,
Thy goodly armor thus hath cost thy life.
Now is my day's work done. I'll take my breath.

---

5 *Empale him* fence him in 6 *fellest* deadliest; *execute* make use of 10 *'Loo*
halloo (hunting call) 11–12 *has the game* wins 12 *'ware horns* beware of
horns
V.8 Battlefield 1 *putrefied core* hard center of an abscess

Rest, sword, thou hast thy fill of blood and death.
   [Begins to disarm.]
   Enter Achilles and his Myrmidons.

ACHILLES
   Look, Hector, how the sun begins to set,
   How ugly night comes breathing at his heels.
   Even with the vail and dark'ning of the sun,   7
   To close the day up, Hector's life is done.

HECTOR
   I am unarmed. Forgo this vantage, Greek.

ACHILLES
   Strike, fellows, strike! This is the man I seek.   10
    [Hector falls.]
   So, Ilion, fall thou next! Come, Troy, sink down!
   Here lies thy heart, thy sinews, and thy bone.
   On, Myrmidons, and cry you all amain,   13
   "Achilles hath the mighty Hector slain!"
    Retreat.
   Hark, a retire upon our Grecian part.   15

GREEK
   The Trojan trumpets sound the like, my lord.

ACHILLES
   The dragon wing of night o'erspreads the earth,
   And, stickler-like, the armies separates.   18
   My half-supped sword, that frankly would have fed,   19
   Pleased with this dainty bait, thus goes to bed.   20
    [Sheathes his sword.]
   Come, tie his body to my horse's tail;
   Along the field I will the Trojan trail.   *Exeunt.*

*

---

7 *vail* setting   13 *amain* loudly   15 *retire* withdrawal   18 *stickler-like* like an umpire in a contest   19 *frankly* freely   20 *bait* morsel, bite

∾ **V.9** *Enter Agamemnon, Ajax, Menelaus, Nestor,*
Diomed, and the rest, marching. [Sound retreat.
Shout.]

AGAMEMNON
  Hark, hark, what shout is that?
NESTOR   Peace, drums!
SOLDIERS *Within*   Achilles!
  Achilles! Hector's slain! Achilles!
DIOMEDES
3 The bruit is, Hector's slain, and by Achilles.
AJAX
  If it be so, yet bragless let it be;
  Great Hector was as good a man as he.
AGAMEMNON
  March patiently along. Let one be sent
  To pray Achilles see us at our tent.
  If in his death the gods have us befriended,
  Great Troy is ours, and our sharp wars are ended.
                                        Exeunt.

*

∾ **V.10** *Enter Aeneas, Paris, Antenor, and Deiphobus.*

AENEAS
  Stand, ho! Yet are we masters of the field.
  Never go home; here starve we out the night.
    Enter Troilus.
TROILUS
  Hector is slain.
ALL   Hector! The gods forbid!
TROILUS
  He's dead, and at the murderer's horse's tail,
5 In beastly sort, dragged through the shameful field.

V.9 Battlefield **3** *bruit* rumor
  V.10 Battlefield **5** *In beastly sort* (1) in inhuman manner, (2) like an
animal

Frown on, you heavens, effect your rage with speed!   6
Sit, gods, upon your thrones, and smile at Troy!   7
I say, at once let your brief plagues be mercy,   8
And linger not our sure destructions on!

AENEAS
My lord, you do discomfort all the host.   10

TROILUS
You understand me not that tell me so.
I do not speak of flight, of fear, of death,
But dare all imminence that gods and men   13
Address their dangers in. Hector is gone.
Who shall tell Priam so, or Hecuba?
Let him that will a screech owl aye be called   16
Go in to Troy, and say there Hector's dead.
There is a word will Priam turn to stone,
Make wells and Niobes of the maids and wives,   19
Cold statues of the youth, and, in a word,   20
Scare Troy out of itself. [But march away.
Hector is dead;] there is no more to say.
Stay yet. You vile abominable tents,
Thus proudly pight upon our Phrygian plains,   24
Let Titan rise as early as he dare,   25
I'll through and through you! And, thou great-sized   26
    coward,
No space of earth shall sunder our two hates.   27
I'll haunt thee like a wicked conscience still,   28
That moldeth goblins swift as frenzy's thoughts.   29
Strike a free march to Troy. With comfort go;   30
Hope of revenge shall hide our inward woe.

---

6 *effect your rage with speed* send down your destruction quickly   7 *smile* i.e.,
in derision   8 *let . . . mercy* show mercy by destroying us quickly   13–14
dare . . . in defy whatever imminent dangers gods or men are preparing   16
aye forever   19 *Niobes* (Niobe, in Greek mythology, was turned to stone but
still wept for the death of her seven sons and seven daughters)   20 *Cold statues* frozen effigies   24 *pight* pitched   25 *Titan* the sun   26 *great-sized coward* i.e., Achilles   27 *sunder* separate   28 *still* continuously   29 *moldeth
goblins* shapes terrifying, demonic apparitions; *frenzy's* madness's   30 *free
march* quick march

Enter Pandarus.

PANDARUS
  But hear you, hear you!

TROILUS
33 Hence, broker-lackey! Ignomy and shame
  Pursue thy life, and live aye with thy name.

                              Exeunt all but Pandarus.

PANDARUS   A goodly medicine for my aching bones! O
  world, world! Thus is the poor agent despised. O trai-
37 tors and bawds, how earnestly are you set a-work, and
  how ill requited! Why should our endeavor be so loved,
  and the performance so loathed? What verse for it?
40 What instance for it? Let me see.
41   Full merrily the humblebee doth sing,
            Till he hath lost his honey and his sting;
43   And being once subdued in armèd tail,
            Sweet honey and sweet notes together fail.
45 Good traders in the flesh, set this in your painted
  cloths:
47 As many as be here of Pandar's hall,
48 Your eyes, half out, weep out at Pandar's fall;
  Or if you cannot weep, yet give some groans,
50 Though not for me, yet for your aching bones.
51 Brethren and sisters of the hold-door trade,
  Some two months hence my will shall here be made.
  It should be now, but that my fear is this,
54 Some gallèd goose of Winchester would hiss.
55 Till then I'll sweat and seek about for eases,
  And at that time bequeath you my diseases.   *[Exit.]*

---

33 *broker-lackey* pander; *Ignomy* ignominy   37 *bawds* whoremongers   40
instance illustration   41 *humblebee* bumblebee   43 *armèd tail* tail with a
sting in it   45 *painted cloths* painted wall hangings   47 *hall* company   48
half out already half blinded with tears   51 *hold-door trade* prostitution   54
gallèd goose of Winchester diseased prostitute (many brothels were located in
the diocese of Winchester when the play was written); *hiss* i.e., with disap-
proval, as if in a theater audience   55 *sweat* take a steam-bath cure (common
treatment for syphilis in Shakespeare's time); *eases* ways of alleviating my suffering

FOR THE BEST IN PAPERBACKS, LOOK FOR THE Ⓟ

In every corner of the world, on every subject under the sun, Penguin represents quality and variety—the very best in publishing today.

For complete information about books available from Penguin—including Puffins, Penguin Classics, and Compass—and how to order them, write to us at the appropriate address below. Please note that for copyright reasons the selection of books varies from country to country.

In the United Kingdom: Please write to *Dept. EP, Penguin Books Ltd, Bath Road, Harmondsworth, West Drayton, Middlesex UB7 0DA.*

In the United States: Please write to *Penguin Putnam Inc., P.O. Box 12289 Dept. B, Newark, New Jersey 07101-5289* or call 1-800-788-6262.

In Canada: Please write to *Penguin Books Canada Ltd, 10 Alcorn Avenue, Suite 300, Toronto, Ontario M4V 3B2.*

In Australia: Please write to *Penguin Books Australia Ltd, P.O. Box 257, Ringwood, Victoria 3134.*

In New Zealand: Please write to *Penguin Books (NZ) Ltd, Private Bag 102902, North Shore Mail Centre, Auckland 10.*

In India: Please write to *Penguin Books India Pvt Ltd, 11 Panchsheel Shopping Centre, Panchsheel Park, New Delhi 110 017.*

In the Netherlands: Please write to *Penguin Books Netherlands bv, Postbus 3507, NL-1001 AH Amsterdam.*

In Germany: Please write to *Penguin Books Deutschland GmbH, Metzlerstrasse 26, 60594 Frankfurt am Main.*

In Spain: Please write to *Penguin Books S. A., Bravo Murillo 19, 1° B, 28015 Madrid.*

In Italy: Please write to *Penguin Italia s.r.l., Via Benedetto Croce 2, 20094 Corsico, Milano.*

In France: Please write to *Penguin France, Le Carré Wilson, 62 rue Benjamin Baillaud, 31500 Toulouse.*

In Japan: Please write to *Penguin Books Japan Ltd, Kaneko Building, 2-3-25 Koraku, Bunkyo-Ku, Tokyo 112.*

In South Africa: Please write to *Penguin Books South Africa (Pty) Ltd, Private Bag X14, Parkview, 2122 Johannesburg.*